Ivan Margolius

Automobiles

WILEY-ACADEMY

In memory of my grandparents, in whose generation the automobile was invented.

First published in Great Britain in 2000 by
WILEY-ACADEMY

 A division of
JOHN WILEY & SONS
Baffins Lane
Chichester
West Sussex PO19 1UD
ISBN: 0 471 60786 X

Other Wiley Editorial Offices
New York • Weinheim • Brisbane • Singapore • Toronto

Design & Art Direction: Alun Evans & Katy Hepburn

Printed and bound in Italy

Contents

Introduction **5**

The Automobile as an Artistic Creation **9**

Architects as Designers of Automotive Objects **32**

Architecture and the Automobile **134**

Notes **154**

Select Bibliography **157**

Acknowledgements **158**

Index **159**

The bodywork of an elegant automobile, standing in front of architect Kotera's buildings, corresponds to the building in its proportions, lines, functional use of materials etc; both are products of the same modern spirit, which has transformed mass into new forms, responding practically to new needs, aesthetically satisfying this spirit's goal of beautiful form adhering to function.

Jaromír Krejcar, 'Jan Kotera', *Zivot II*, 1922

I think that cars today are almost the exact equivalent of the great Gothic cathedrals: I mean the supreme creation of an era, conceived with passion by unknown artists, and consumed in image if not in usage by a whole population which appropriates them as a purely magical object.

Roland Barthes, 'The New Citroën', *Mythologies*, 1957

Now that would be a challenge, to design a car as flexible as the horse.

Peter Rice, *An Engineer Imagines*, 1992

Look after goodness and truth, and beauty will take care of herself.

Quoted by Barnes N Wallis in his Royal Designers for Industry address, 1963

Introduction

Man has always searched for congenial objects to include in his personal environment so as to expand and enrich his existence. In the twentieth century, the deep relationship between man and his horse has been transferred to a new, almost equally dependable and indispensable friend – the automobile. We may know and understand our cars better than any human being, and often spend happier times with them than with our families. The automobile can be our closest companion; one that we desire passionately, love faithfully and, when it is gone, remember with nostalgia.

A house – a static object – is for its owner an expression of individuality, family security, durability and standing in society; a reflection of taste, an investment. The automobile, when it began to be available, was an exciting addition to the static dwelling, representing speed, progress, glamour, adventure, a courageous and pioneering spirit. It seemed to extend one's body and space, it introduced new skills; it improved lifestyle and allowed its owner to imitate other people's status. The car permanently altered people's lives, affording them movement instead of immobility. The more affluent society grew, the more mobile it became.

It may seem extraordinary that architects – designers of stationary objects – should concern themselves with automobile design. However, the automobile has long touched their imaginations, appearing to them as a house on wheels, as mobile accommodation. When the motor-driven vehicle was invented, architects recognised that its image, form and function would affect the quality of people's lives and their surroundings. Architects are, by training and by their very nature, fascinated not only by progress and the impact of technology on building design and construction, but also by other technical, engineering and artistic spheres of human activity. Moreover, architectural education trains them as designers to reconcile all aspects of man's practical and emotional attitudes to the environment. This develops in them a deep understanding of human aspirations and desires, of lifestyles and trends, of the ever-changing scene of human existence.

On the surface, there is very little to compare between automobile and architectural design. Architectural design almost always starts from a blank sheet of paper, because a building's design is usually specific to factors such as site, purpose and situation. There are regulations, fire-prevention and safety measures, planning directives, building standards and codes, cost, structural, ergonomic and environmental criteria to follow, and past and present architectural styles to consider. However, the design of a building is flexible enough to allow an individual approach to each problem. It is each architect's desire to produce a personal, original answer to the client's brief and that is why there are no two building designs exactly alike.[1] Architects design a prototype every time they propose a building: components are put together in new ways each time, and new solutions to problems are found. The car industry works in the opposite way. There are given safety criteria and complex requirements concerning structure, engine size and performance, comfort, aesthetics, fuel economy, production and so on that remain basically unaltered from model to model. If a new design is to be launched, it is usually based on the previous line of component and design development to reduce the enormous costs involved in re-tooling the production line. Once a prototype is produced (which might take several years of research, development and testing, unlike architecture where there are only a few months, or sometimes days, to prepare drawings for construction), the car goes into mass-production and large numbers of units are distributed for marketing. This does not mean that the car industry cannot make fast decisions: it carries out experiments in racing and rallying, which act as testing grounds for innovations. If suitable and appropriate, these innovations are then transferred to mass-produced passenger cars.

The structure of a car needs to respond positively to the dynamic environment of movement, should be sufficiently stiff in torsion, and stable enough at sudden braking points and in bends. The smooth surface and structure of the car body can form a single-element integral shell (known as monocoque) or can be treated as separate elements with composite structural action. The car body has to be shaped to cope with air penetration and the aesthetic requirements of expressing movement. It must function safely and be weatherproof. Just as architecture involves many technical, environmental and human aspects fused into a single design, so a car combines many mechanical, ergonomic and safety requirements. One significant respect in which automobile design may differ from the expression of architectural form is in the play of surfaces and light. The car's polished metal or shiny paint reflects light and shade, and enhances form and contours.

Car design has evolved from multiple directions and it is not easy to describe it in coherent stages. Like other new machines, automobiles have no past connections, tradition or ties, not only because of their short history but also because of the constant necessity to advance and compete in the marketplace. As the architecture critic Martin Pawley has written, 'The car is the best example of continuous product evolution in the history of technology.'[2] As architecture has developed in a linear manner, from style to style, picking up influences through time, it is possible to search backwards for inspiration. In architecture, one can turn back the clock, as the various classical and gothic revivals, and most recently, postmodernism, have shown. However, the progress of automobile design is impossible to reverse. We can return to the Model T Ford no more than we can return to the Middle Ages.

In his 1932 article 'The Automobile Standard and Artistic Creation', Walter Gropius discussed the varied possibilities of the car designer's art: 'Nowadays designers lay stress on the essential research, on understanding the function of those objects, which are to be created, and they use the specific laws of form-making – that is, laws of rhythm, proportion, of light-dark contrast, of balance and of the full and empty space – adopting them logically to the technical procedures used by the engineer ... As an example: our aim is to give the car a long, extended look. From the absolute point of view of fashioning the obvious solution is – and often it is done that way – to design the roof of the body as low as possible. However, with that will suffer the comfort inside the car and entry into it. Therefore the designer has to use his skills and with other means make an impression that the car body is longer, for example by seemingly optically stretching the bonnet. This he can achieve also by extending the paintwork from the side views of the car almost on to the plane of the radiator. He should avoid lengthening vertical lines, and finally enlarge the width of windows and introduce horizontal lines in the body to organise the play of light on the paintwork.'[3]

Arthur Drexler, curator at the Museum of Modern Art in New York, tried to define the art of car body design in his introduction to the 'Ten Automobiles' exhibition held at the museum in 1953. 'The aesthetic merits of an automobile depend not on methods by which it is produced, but on the designer's mastery of sculptural problems. These problems of sculptural form have to do with the ways in which a volume may be defined. Like the exterior wall of a house, the metal shell of an automobile takes its shape from the space it envelops. Details on the surface of this shell, like the details on the façade of a house, can suggest by their shape and location the nature of the space enclosed. But, unlike a house, an automobile moves, and we expect an indication from its shape as to the direction its passengers face and the location of its wheels.'[4]

As for the inside of the car, Drexler observed that 'the interiors of American cars are often designed to duplicate in domestic comfort the living room of the driver's home'.[5] More than thirty years later, British design critic Stephen Bayley was of the same opinion: 'Inside a car you get a perfect little exercise in interior design, a controlled environment more perfect than most homes.'[6] Indeed, there was a further advantage, as Le Corbusier remarked after visiting the Ford factory in Detroit and seeing the production of the Model A:'When I, an architect, pay 10,000 francs to a contractor it does not even cover the cost of one room. Yet here for 10,000 francs Ford delivers the marvellous car that we all know.'[7]

Because of their flexible and open-minded approach to design, architects can be the ideal professionals to guide the car industry. In 1978, for example, the architect Renzo Piano – with engineer Peter Rice – was asked by Fiat to find solutions, resolve design problems, and introduce new ideas into the company's development programme. While car-makers can learn from architects, so architecture can learn from car design. In 1926, Theo van Doesburg wrote that 'presently building is already gradually assuming the characteristics of an assembly line; the assembling of normalised, machine-produced parts. Just like our cars (Ford, Fiat, Citroën etc), our dwellings will be factory-produced within the foreseeable future ... in the same manner as mass-produced articles, in the grand industrial way.'[8] It took over seventy years for architects to realise this fully. In 1999, the multidisciplinary British practice Ove Arup invested in acquiring an automotive design company, Design Research Associates Limited, to bring expertise from the automobile industry into architecture in order to help to develop prefabricated building systems.

Le Corbusier believed that architects should study engineer-designed machines such as automobiles and aeroplanes and their construction in order to find standards on which to base modern architectural principles, and that this would point the way forwards for modern architecture. He argued that 'houses must go up all of a piece, made by machine tools in a factory, assembled as Ford assembles cars on moving conveyor belts.'[9] For him, an aeroplane was a little house that could fly and resist the storm. It was, he said, in an aircraft factory that the soldier-architects decided to build houses like aircraft, with the same structural methods, lightweight framing, metal bracing and tubular supports.

In his book *Vers une architecture* (*Towards a New Architecture*), Le Corbusier described houses as machines for living in. For him, machines were manifestations not burdened or compromised by tradition and historical inheritance. They were symbols of the future, of things to come. He used examples of motorcars, aeroplanes and steamships to illustrate how progress within that specific technical design field should influence the art of architecture. He compared the Parthenon, which represented the culmination of classical architecture, to automobile design. His intention was to implant early on the notion that a direct connection exists between machines and buildings. In this way, he tried to influence future architects' views of the technical world by helping them to encompass in their thinking and their designs the progress achieved in other fields of human endeavour.

Le Corbusier was one of a number of well-known architects who liked to pair the architecture of their houses with their favourite automobiles in order to illustrate the synthesis of architecture and automobile design, and to emphasise the close functional and aesthetic relationship between them. He included cars in perspective views and photographed his completed buildings with his Voisin motorcar carefully parked in front – the result being a harmonising composition of the two elements, stressing their close affinity. Similarly, Frank Lloyd Wright believed that his cars had to 'look becoming to' his architecture, reinforcing the close bond most architects feel between their architectural design and their automobiles.

The Automobile as an Artistic Creation

Architects love automobiles. Automobiles attract many people, but there seems to be a special bond between architects and cars. Since the earliest days of the motorcar, architects have realised that to propose an automobile is an opportunity for an exercise in miniature architecture, the design of a detachable mobile room. It is a way for them to perfect the synthesis of art, design and the latest technology.

Cars are complex objects, microcosms of creative endeavour, behavioural patterns, and cultural and technological developments. These interactive mobile environments have had a great impact on the history and progress of humanity. The cars we see today will without doubt become obsolete within several decades due to severe environmental pressures – such as the amount of land taken up by roads and parking spaces, and pollution from engine emissions. However, with the invention of new fuels and energy supplies, some form of personal, individual transport will doubtless continue. 'Architecture on wheels' is here to stay. No other product has become so firmly embedded in the language and behaviour of our society as the motorcar, symbolising, by its constantly changing form, the continuous progress of technology as well as the illusions and myths of the modern world.

Popular Attitudes to the Automobile

What does a motorcar mean to different people? According to one American survey, the choice of a car can reflect one's personal philosophy and position in society. For example, the university professor tends to disclose, sometimes unwillingly, a subconscious leaning towards conservatism by buying large, solid, showy cars; the liberal assistant professor, meanwhile, loves smart, sexy, European imports; and the radical thinkers would rather walk than own a car.[10] On the other side of the Atlantic, the French, Italians and Germans prefer cars made in their own countries. The British, however, tend to make their choice depending on the size of their pockets or the depth of their passion. Indeed, owners develop many important and sometimes conflicting attitudes in relation to their automobiles; listed in somewhat dispassionate form, these might include the motorcar viewed as:

an easily operable mechanical unit allowing personal mobility and travel;

a moving object with an appropriate, safe external envelope enclosing a comfortable, well-designed interior;

a product manufactured by advanced production processes, providing employment for a large number of people;

an example of complex industrial design with world-wide mass-production and distribution;

an object that can be bought economically and traded successfully;

a place of demise – in many cases.

So with a list of such practical concerns in mind, why do we love the car so much? How does it arouse such passion? The answers are many:

it provides the excitement of speed, power and the release of aggression;

it gives us a sense of control over our own destiny;

it bolsters our self-esteem, and our personal and national pride;

it provides a place for reflection and motivation;

it offers the freedom of the road, the romance of travel, and the extension of our house, of our personal space;

it offers expression and advertisement of the owner's personality, social status, brand loyalty and sophistication;

it is a place for closeness, intimacy and accommodation, a realm of privacy within the public domain;

it is a beautiful object full of mystery, eroticism and inspiration;

it is an object of cultural expression and the symbol of an era.

In his 1880 book *La maison à vapeur*, the French writer Jules Verne was already predicting not only the versatility of automobiles but, significantly, the psychology of drivers and their emotional relationships with the car '... the modern car ... What a dream! To stop when one wishes, carry along when one pleases, to walk, to stroll, or gallop, if one likes, to carry along not only one's bedroom but also one's salon, dining room, smoking room, and of course one's kitchen and cook – there's progress.'[11]

Early Architectural Interest in the Automobile

For architects to extend their skills to the design of these fantastic vehicles was a natural progression. In earlier times, architects had been seen as artisans and craftsmen, all-round designers, not only of buildings but also of utilitarian objects, *objets d'art*, textiles, jewellery, furniture, light fittings, ironmongery, even tombs. Not until Walter Dorwin Teague, Raymond Loewy, Henry Dreyfuss, Norman Bel Geddes, Harold van Doren and others established industrial design as an independent profession in the late 1920s did architecture lose its leading edge as the mother of arts, because 'architecture could no longer be considered the legitimate, total expression of the taste of the age'.[12] Some architects, however, understood the changing conditions of the design environment and strove to become involved again not only in building and construction but in other fields of design. The design of the car was an ideal opportunity to reclaim their all-round creativity.

Architects had, of course, developed an interest in the evolution of automotive design much earlier than this. Leonardo da Vinci made sketches for a spring-driven wagon in 1478 and for a scythed vehicle and a war machine in 1483. A few centuries later, Josef Aloysius Hansom, architect and editor of *The Builder* magazine, invented the horse-driven cab (1834), which was named after him. Then, in 1906, as mechanical locomotion came to replace horse-drawn vehicles on the roads, the Austrian architect Josef Maria Olbrich designed a car body for Opel. In 1914, fellow Austrian Josef Hoffmann proposed an automobile for Alexander Pazzani, general director of Poldi Hütte in Bohemia (though so far no details of this design have been uncovered). Between 1927 and 1936, Hoffmann also conceived train interiors for the Simmering Railroad Carriage Factory in Vienna, using perforated metal sheeting and corrugated aluminium as wall coverings. Even the celebrated British architect Sir Edwin Lutyens could not resist the attraction of vehicle design, proposing a fantastic royal state limousine (1921-1924) – possibly to complement his Queen Mary's Dolls' House – which had wheels with rubber tyres.

Of course, no wheel exists in nature and its invention has had an unprecedented effect on our development

Leonardo da Vinci: design for a four-wheel military machine, c. 1483. (Copyright of the British Museum) Medieval design with very 'modern' body form. Roger Bacon (1214-1294) predicted that one of the elements that would make mankind great would be the possibility of the easy transport of people and goods in wagons not pulled by any animal and driven with an incredible speed.

Sir Edwin Lutyens: design for a royal state limousine (1921-24). This fantastic creation displays a modern element in the choice of wheels, which have rubber tyres. (British Architectural Library, RIBA, London)

and progress. Initially, pairs of wheels were assembled to create wagons and carts that were pulled by humans and later by tamed animals. Only when the steam engine was invented did men such as Nicolaus-Joseph Cugnot (in 1769-71), Richard Trevithick (in 1798-1801) and Oliver Evans (in 1805), attempt to build self-propelled vehicles. However, since the steam engine was heavy and awkward, work began to replace it with a less clumsy and lighter power unit that would move a flexible and easy-to-handle road vehicle. The invention of the gas engine by Jean Joseph Etienne Lenoir and Nikolaus August Otto in the 1860s established the principles of the internal combustion motor that helped Karl Benz, Gottlieb Daimler and Wilhelm Maybach to power their three- and four-wheel carriages twenty years later. When the combustion engine was created and used for the horseless carriage, a number of people in both the technical and artistic worlds felt that human society had entered a new stage of development from which it could never turn back.

It was on New Year's Eve , 1879, that Karl Benz resumed work on the prototype of his two-stroke combustion engine, a project on which he had been labouring without much success but with a good deal of encouragement from his wife Bertha. As he and Bertha stood in front of the engine, contemplating it as if it were a great mystery, a riddle impossible to solve, Karl turned the crank lever once more. Suddenly the engine burst into a 'put-put-put' and the music of the future resounded with a regular rhythm in their ears. Fascinated, they listened to it for a full hour, never tiring of its monotonous song. When the church bells began to sound, they rang in not just the new year, but the coming of a new era.

Cultural Reactions to the Automobile

The Belgian architect Henry van der Velde demonstrated that he understood the impact of this new rhythm when, in 1907, he discussed the existence of a universal force residing in all things man-made as well as natural, even in machine parts. This universal force, he argued, springs from what is the cleanest, most powerful element of our being, from a passion that binds us in a direct relationship with the innermost being of all things: from rhythm. In his poem 'La Petite Auto', the French poet Guillaume Apollinaire marked not only the beginning of the First World War but also the revolution that the car brought for mankind:

Within myself I sensed new beings full of dexterity
Building up and organising a new universe
A shopkeeper of untold wealth and prodigious size
Was arranging an extraordinary display-window
And gigantic shepherds were leading
Great dumb herds that browsed on words
And around whom all the dogs in the road were barking
And passing that afternoon by Fontainebleau
We arrived in Paris
At the moment when the mobilisation posters were going up
And my comrade and I understood then
That the little motorcar had brought us into a new epoch
And though we were both mature men
We had just been born. [13]

In the 'Futurist Manifesto' published in *Le Figaro* on 20 February 1909, the Italian poet Filippo Tommaso Marinetti expressed the brutal excitement of speed and danger aroused by this new machine. 'We declare that a new beauty has enriched the splendour of the earth: the beauty of speed. A racing car with its bonnet adorned with giant tubes, serpents of explosive breath ... a roaring automobile, which seems to run on grapeshot is more beautiful than the Victory of Samothrace.' [14]

In 1914, in his *Architettura futurista manifesto* (first published in 1972), another Futurist, the painter Umberto Boccioni, described in a very advanced way the influence of the new machines on the art of architecture. 'Ships, cars, railway stations have attained even greater aesthetic expression the more they have subordinated their architectural design to the needs they were designed to meet. The great railway sheds that were distantly related to the grandiose naves of cathedrals have been succeeded by simple roofs, sufficient and necessary for arriving and departing trains. The masts, the high smoke stacks, which connected ships to plants in flower, that is, to the irregularity of nature, have disappeared to make way for a necessary whole: cutting ellipsoidal planes, penetrating, designed to avoid friction. Automobiles have reduced the dimensions that connected them to

Umberto Boccioni: this dynamic and exciting cover of Avanti della Domenica, *1905, preceded FT Marinetti's 'Futurist Manifesto by four years. (*Architectural Design)

Marcel Duchamp: The Bride Stripped Bare by Her Bachelors, Even *(Large Glass), 1915-23, replica, with Richard Hamilton, 1965-66. (Tate Gallery, London)*

carriages and diligence. The care taken to develop motors razes them to the ground and arranges them like bullets. A time will come when air machines no longer imitate birds and fish, always getting nearer to the forms dictated by the need for stability and speed.'[15]

Francis Picabia, the French painter and maker of films such as *Entr'acte (Interval)*,[16] was fanatical about cars, owning scores of automobiles. He even had a racing car attached to a radial arm on top of a tower so that as he spun round in it he could observe the ever-circling countryside. His object-portraits included a camera, an electric lamp and automobile parts such as a spark plug and a carburettor. He believed that the machine had become more than a mere *adjunct* of life – it was part of human life, perhaps its very soul. For Picabia, the machine represented the spirit of modernity and humanity. It also became a reflection of human psychology and sexual behaviour. Picabia put man's invention of the machine on a level with God's creation of man.

Objects of Desire and Destruction

Marcel Duchamp was a friend of Picabia's and the two men often exchanged views on art, influencing each other's work. In October 1912, they travelled with Guillaume Apollinaire from Paris to the Jura mountains to stay in an old fortified farmhouse belonging to Gabrielle Buffet, Picabia's wife. They made the journey in Picabia's five-cylinder automobile driven by his chauffeur, Victor. The trip greatly affected Duchamp, inspiring him between 1915 and 1923 to create *The Bride Stripped Bare By Her Bachelors, Even (Large Glass)*. On his return, Duchamp noted: 'The machine with five hearts, the pure child of nickel and platinum, must dominate the Jura-Paris road.'[17] *Large Glass* symbolised a machine transferred into the human world of relationships and indicated explicit sexuality. Duchamp imagined that the 'bride' was a virginal machine, a motor of very feeble cylinder power, a superficial instrument activated by the fuel of love and electric sparks. The bachelor-machine, meanwhile, was fat and lustful and had a motor of desire, which was separated from the bride by a cooler with blades. The picture portrayed a mechanism that conveyed the unfolding of the bride, who wanted to be stripped bare, and a similar ecstasy in the bachelor achieving his desire.

In the avant-garde art magazine *219*, run by the American photographer and impresario Alfred Stieglitz, Paul Haviland confirmed the sexual aspect of machines and explained their appeal: 'Man made the machine in his own image. She has limbs, which act; lungs, which breathe; a heart, which beats; a nervous system through which runs electricity ... The machine is his "daughter born without a mother". That is why he loves her.'[18] Picabia too – possibly at Duchamp's suggestion – called several of his machine paintings *Fille née sans mère* (1915, 1917).

In his book *Là-Bas* (1891), the French novelist Joris-Karl Huysmans also described the sexual aspect of machines: 'Look at the machine, the play of pistons in the cylinders: they are steel Romeos inside cast-iron Juliets. The ways of human expression are in no way different to the back-and-forth of our machines. This is a law to which one must pay homage, unless one is either impotent or a saint.'[19] Marinetti's poem 'To the Automobile' (1905) also celebrates an intimate union of man and his machine during a car journey. The driver tells his car, 'I am at your mercy ... Take me! ... I become inflamed with the fever and desire of the steely breaths from your nostrils!'[20]

Given this sexual connection with machines, it is not surprising that many men regard cars as female and that their sexual fantasies include automotive machines – something filmmakers and advertising agencies have been quick to exploit. Ironically, car advertisers sometimes turn to architecture to enhance the latest automobile designs, using buildings created by famous architects as backdrops to symbolise modernity, power and wealth, and to show that the car is keeping up with the newest developments in arts and fashion.

Like many other larger-than-life machines, cars also have their destructive side. Automobiles kill. Many of the reasons given by some for their love and fascination with automobiles are, for others, reasons for hating them. They can be seen as objects bringing misery, danger and destruction. Among those who have died in automobile accidents there have been many icons. In November 1950, Pierre-Jules Boulanger was killed while testing a development prototype of the Citroën DS19, smashing into a tree after skidding on a straight road near Brout-Vernet. Five years later, the actor James Dean died in the California desert in a Porsche 550 Spyder. The painter Jackson Pollock crashed while driving his 1950 Oldsmobile convertible on Long Island in 1956. In 1960, the French writer Albert Camus was killed in Facel Vega near Pont-sur-Yonne in France, driven by his publisher Michel Gallimard. Princess Grace of Monaco, the former actress Grace Kelly, came off the road near La Turbie in her Rover 3500 P5B in September 1982. Perhaps the most publicised and mourned fatal car crash took place on the last day of August 1997 when Princess Diana, Dodi Fayed and their driver were killed in a Mercedes-Benz S280 limousine in Paris.

A Metaphor for Modernity

However, despite their terrible destructive potential, cars have become an accepted part of daily life. John Steinbeck wrote in *Cannery Row* (1945) that the Model T Ford, manufactured in large numbers and accessible to many, had a greater influence on the American way of life than any other machine. 'Someone should write an erudite essay on the moral, physical and aesthetic effect of the Model T Ford on the American nation. Two generations of Americans knew more about the Ford coil than the clitoris, about the planetary system of gears than the solar system of stars. With the Model T, part of the concept of private property disappeared. Pliers ceased to be privately owned and a tyre pump belonged to the last man who had picked it up. Most of the babies of the period were conceived in Model T Fords and not a few were born in them.'[21]

After witnessing the launch of the Italian sculptor Flaminio Bertoni's new Citroën DS19 at the Paris Autosalon in autumn 1955, Roland Barthes, the French professor, scholar and critic, compared it to that great architectural achievement, so revered in France: the Gothic cathedral. Both, he argued, represented the same aesthetic value and were results of comparable intellectual effort; both were artistic masterpieces. The Citroën encapsulated a new image, 'the beginnings of a new phenomenology of assembling, as if one progressed from a world where elements are welded to a world where they juxtaposed and hold together by sole virtue of their wondrous

The Citroën DS19 being unveiled to astonished crowds at the 1955 Salon de l'Automobile, Paris. (Citroën)

shape'.[22] Barthes was convinced that the new Citroën represented a humanised art, marking a change in the mythology of cars. 'Until now, the ultimate in cars belonged rather to the bestiary of power; here it becomes at once more spiritual and more object-like, it is now more homely, more attuned to this sublimation of the utensil ... the small levers topped by a white ball, the very simple dials, the very discreteness of nickel-work, all this signifies a kind of control exercised over motion, which is henceforth conceived as comfort rather than performance. One is obviously turning from alchemy of speed to a relish in driving.'[23]

In their writings and arguments, architects, artists and architectural historians have used the automobile as an archetypal symbol of a utilitarian machine that directly embodies functionality and rationality and at the same time arouses aesthetic reaction. They have used it as a gauge to judge, criticise and confront the progress of contemporary architecture with the development of modern technology. At the beginning of the twentieth century, it was acknowledged that machinery was a new element in the human environment and a new spirit of the coming era. It soon became obvious that it could be an example of creativity embracing the latest technology and methods of production. At the same time, the transformation from manual to machine production at the end of nineteenth century inspired new developments in arts and industry. The machine became the essential vehicle of modern form when mass-production replaced craft and manual skill. New artistic trends elevated the inherent formal beauty of the machine by abstracting aesthetic elements from the machine world and applying them to art. The automobile was regarded as the typical machine to source design ideas, a metaphor for modernity and progress.

Pop art painter Richard Hamilton, writing with art historian Lawrence Gowing, summarised the role of the machine and its great importance to man, to progress and evolution: 'The devices, which man makes to extend his physical potentialities are the oldest and newest things we know about him.'[24] Hamilton and Gowing recognised that machines acted as extensions to the human senses. Tools and weapons added to the natural power of the hand and the later additions of mechanical, optical, electric and electronic inventions helped man master the world.

Utility and Beauty

Peter Behrens, the German architect and industrial designer, believed that 'architecture is the art of building, and combines in its name two ideas, the mastery of the practical, and the art of the beautiful. There is something exhilarating in being able to combine in one word the two ideas – that of practical utility and that of abstract beauty – which unfortunately have too often been opposed to each other ... The practical object does not seem to us to be any longer entirely subservient to mere utility, but combines therewith a certain degree of pleasure. Efforts were made formerly to relieve the bareness of everyday utility by embellishing it, adding ornaments to plain, serviceable objects and hiding the mere prosaic purpose ... Then came the realisation of physical pleasure existing in the useful and the suitable, and by degrees, people wanted to see the intention, to observe the suitability of things ... This development of artistic perception, combined with the progress made in our technique and newly discovered materials, is at once a guarantee of the fertility of the modern style and its justification.'[25]

By 1910, the German writer Joseph-August Lux was already suggesting in his book *Ingenieur-Aesthetik* that what distinguished his era from earlier civilisations was that it took its distinctive artistic character exclusively from machines. In the past, it had been different: the machines themselves used to be disguised by ornamentation in the contemporary styles. Lux admired the practical style of many of the vehicles that were emerging at the turn of the century and that revealed the influence of the new machine aesthetic. This practical way of thinking had developed vehicles into structures that seemed almost to be endowed with human life. Functionality did not, as had been expected, lead to impersonality. On the contrary, it allowed for extensive personal differentiation. Moreover, Lux believed that civilisation was reflected not in architecture, but in vehicles and modern transport engineering. It was there that we could discover the style of our age.[26]

The idea that mechanical objects evolve functionally towards an ideal form has fascinated artists since the early 1920s. In 1924, the French artist Fernand Léger, whose paintings and sculptural compositions were much influenced by machine technology, wrote an article entitled 'The Machine Aesthetic' for the avant-garde journal *Bulletin de l'Effort Moderne*.[27] Léger's argument – that in the case of the evolution of the automobile, the more the machine perfects its utilitarian functions, the more beautiful it becomes – remains both an inspiration and a challenge for automobile designers, engineers and architects.

Herbert Read argued that industrial design is not concerned with works of art whose sole purpose is to please the senses or the intellect, but with those that, in addition, perform a utilitarian function. Nevertheless, it is false to assume that if an object performs its function in the most efficient way possible, it therefore possesses the necessary aesthetic qualities: art implies values more various than those determined by practical necessity. There is, said Read, a need for the approach of the abstract artist, the artist who arranges materials until they combine the highest degree of 'practical economy' with the greatest measure of spiritual freedom. The most unexpected object – for example a motorcar – can acquire an abstract kind of beauty. Read identified an industrial designer as a designer of abstract, non-representational, non-figurative, forms. For him, design was a function of the abstract artist.[28]

Interestingly, in the first and second editions of *Art and Industry* (published in 1934 and 1944), Read chose to

Two images from Art and Industry *by Herbert Read, 1953 edition, where Read compared the form of Salginatobel Bridge (1929-30) by Robert Maillart with the graceful Bentley Mark VI drop-head coupé (1947-48).*

illustrate his point that beauty and order were inherent in all rationally designed products by comparing two images. He juxtaposed a photograph of a 40-50hp Phantom II Continental Rolls-Royce chassis mounted with a sports foursome coupé designed by Jack Barclay Ltd, and a picture of Robert Maillart's Salginatobel Bridge in Schiers, Switzerland (1929-30). For the third edition of the book, published in 1953, the photograph of the Rolls-Royce was replaced by a streamlined Bentley Mark VI drop-head coupé from 1947-48 (with coachwork by Windover Ltd), more in keeping with Maillart's brilliant bridge design. In an even later edition, Read again changed the car to keep pace with the fast design evolution of automobiles, this time using a 1955 Alvis saloon, bodied by Graber of Berne.

Raymond Loewy, the famous industrial designer, recounted in his autobiography *Never Leave Well Enough Alone* (published in 1951) that automobile design represents industrial design at its highest degree of technical perfection. Such design requires imagination and talent, as well as specialist knowledge. It includes everything from metalwork, instruments, mascots, textiles and rugs, to lighting and acoustics. Good car designers make good industrial designers. Many of Loewy's best designers made their debut in the domain of the automobile. These were true fanatics, unable to think of anything except automobiles. 'You ask them out to dinner, and at the end of the meal the tablecloth is covered with sketches of automobile parts.'[29] (Something they have in common with architects: many winning architectural competitions and buildings were conceived at a restaurant table.)

Some would argue that the automobile, an example of the most advanced product of contemporary technology, has acted as a link between architects and engineers. An automobile is a synthesis of mechanical, structural and spatial requirements, and to be satisfactorily resolved, its design depends on the combined efforts of many professionals whose goal is to achieve an aesthetically pleasing object. In order to exist functionally within our environment, this dynamic object needs roads, bridges, fly-overs, petrol and service stations, and buildings to accommodate it. As a design problem, the automobile has therefore encouraged communication between architects and engineers, professions that had drifted apart during the last century.

In his influential article 'Machine Aesthetics', which appeared in *The Architectural Review* in 1955, Reyner Banham suggested that architects had been frightened of machines ever since engineering established itself as an independent profession.[30] He argued that architecture should learn from and be influenced by machines. To illustrate his point, *The Architectural Review*'s editors chose two pictures of the stunning Bertone coachwork of the Berlinetta Aerodinamica Tecnica BAT7 on the Alfa Romeo 1900 SS chassis designed by Franco Scaglione and developed in 1954. This car design – the most advanced of its time – was achieved after extensive wind-tunnel testing had been carried out to attain the absolute streamlining and stability required for the modern automobile. Interestingly, *The Architectural Review*'s cover carried a contrasting picture of a 1907 Rolls-Royce Silver Ghost. This showed the simple engineering qualities of early automotive design, based on logical and rational functional principles and the structure of the first machine age. Banham argued that already in these early stages of automobile development, the engineering design of machines was in part inspired by artistic influences, and indeed the form of the Rolls-Royce radiator, though it appears to be wholly functional, was

Cover of The Architectural Review *magazine, April 1955. For the first time a highbrow architectural magazine, then edited by JM Richards, displayed a car image on the cover without a building in the background.*

Franco Scaglione: the revolutionary BAT 7 on Alfa Romeo chassis, 1954. Perhaps the most imaginary car body design yet. (Carrozzeria Bertone S.p.A.)

rumoured to be scaled-down from the Parthenon.

A different view was expressed in a reader's observation published in 1927 in the journal *Bulletin de l'Effort Moderne*. While walking down the Champs Elysées in Paris, he saw displayed in a showroom a car with a radiator cap representing a miniature *Victory of Samothrace* (or rather the *Spirit of Ecstasy* by Charles Sykes, RA). It was, he thought, completely ridiculous and quite contrary to the precise, simple and logical order of the car itself. The possible source of inspiration for the radiator design did not occur to him.

In articles in *L'Esprit nouveau*,[31] Le Corbusier and Amédée Ozenfant (under the pseudonym Saugnier) had proposed certain automobiles as standards to be followed in architecture. In 'Machine Aesthetics', Reyner Banham took issue with Le Corbusier's argument, countering that the cars he chose could not set a standard for architecture because they were one-off luxury models rather than mass-produced cars. However, what Le Corbusier meant was that any beautiful, utilitarian machine object – luxury or mass-produced – posed itself as a model for the architect to admire and from which to seek inspiration and guidance. Rather than being frightened of machines, as Banham supposes, many architects are more in awe of them; while they might not want or need to understand them, like Le Corbusier they try to copy their aesthetics and incorporate elements of them into architecture.

Banham also believed that the machine aesthetic had become a defence used by architects who were unable to absorb engineering attitudes and who refused to assimilate the more complex developments in technology. Architects, he claimed, rejected complicated machines for not being the true, simple, utilitarian objects that had initially influenced the development of functionalist architecture.

There were others – critics, writers and painters – who argued that machines designed strictly for utility were inherently pure and beautiful. However, the belief that functionality and utility consistently produce beauty is too elementary. The view that machine objects of maximum utility and the minimum price always display the simplest form is also mistaken, because it does not take into account the pressure of market forces: popular demand may not be satisfied with simplicity and may ask for more complex products, which will then be more saleable. Efforts to satisfy the market may, however, have negative consequences. Tomás Maldonado, an Argentinean painter, teacher and director of the Hochschule für Gestaltung in Ulm, Germany, pointed out in the late 1950s and 1960s that the continuous interaction between needs and objects, between production and consumption, had opened a split between creativity and execution – a situation that could lead to excessive production, causing environmental chaos. Maldonado also believed – mistakenly – that in the past, the product determined to a certain extent the operative behaviour of the machine; in the future, he argued, it would be the operative behaviour of the machine that would determine the product. In this way, machines such as robots would control the design of the product and exclude humans from tinkering with styling.

In the 1930s, Norman Bel Geddes, the prophetic American designer, was forthright about the direct relationship between beauty and function, as well as the misuse of ornaments in industrial design. 'Ornament, in such forms as decorative cornices, horizontal bands, part of them way up the structure and more along the base, has been considered necessary as a relief to the eye. Architects, having been schooled in materials and principles permitting such views and consequently believing in them, will tell you that the public would be unhappy if such ornamentation were not employed. Designers of automobiles, who have not been able to free themselves from the precedent of the horseless carriage or coach, take much the same view in their work. How out of place the moulding and gadgets that we see on our automobile, even of the smartest type, would appear if we saw them on an airplane! When the airplane was developed, it was an all new problem. Its requirements were such that it never occurred to anyone to base its design principles on, for instance, a carriage with wings. One may say that when the design of an object is in keeping with the purpose it serves, it appeals to us as having a distinctive kind of beauty. That is why we are impressed by the stirring beauty of airplanes.'[32]

Today, Norman Foster believes that pure adherence to functionality is not enough: 'There is a common misconception about architecture and design – the belief that if the forces of nature are allowed to create form then that form will be automatically beautiful (the "if it looks right it is right" sort of argument). Personally, I think this is nonsense. There is no doubt that an aircraft is an extreme example, but I cannot believe mere aerodynamics gave this piece of industrial architecture [the Boeing 747] its heroic outer form.'[33]

Le Corbusier wrote in *Vers une architecture* that 'when a thing responds to a need, it is not beautiful; it satisfies all one part of our mind, the primary part, without which there is no possibility of richer satisfactions ... Architecture has another meaning and other ends to pursue than showing construction and responding to needs ... Architecture is the art above all other arts. It achieves a state of platonic grandeur, mathematical order, speculation, the perception of the harmony, which lies in emotional relationships.'[34] In Le Corbusier's view, the problem of the aeroplane and the automobile has been satisfactorily resolved, but the problem of architecture has not yet been stated. In our epoch, once a problem has been properly stated, it finds a solution.

The Question of Style
Le Corbusier correctly identified the problem of architecture when he pointed out that it was the only profession in which progress was not considered necessary and in which the references were always to the past.[35] Automobile design, on the other hand, had to keep up with progress, always looking forward to new ideas and new technologies to survive and succeed.

The Czech architect Jaromír Krejcar, who briefly taught at the Architectural Association in London after the Second World War, was much taken by the power of machines, automobiles and ocean liners, and he set images of automobiles against his proposed buildings. In 1922, he wrote: 'The architecture of the transatlantic liners is an excellent example of modern architecture whose forms, resulting from their very purposefulness as products of modern technology, creatively define the present. The language of these forms is clear, comprehensible to a man thinking in a modern way, and as close to him as is travelling by a modern transatlantic liner in comparison with a galley ... Nowadays, if we want to see works of pure, modern architectural forms, we must return to the objects, which had fortunately been overlooked by art, and which, saved from artful deformation, became what

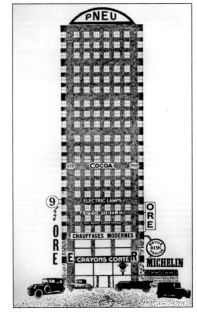

Jaromír Krejcar: proposal for a department store in skyscraper form, 1922. The collage technique is employed to illustrate a busy urban environment.

art used to be in the times of stylistic unity, namely a form of expression of the times. Artistic architecture has been seeking justification for its existence since the time it separated from technology.'[36]

In 1920, the English architect and writer William Lethaby, considering architectural styles in relation to car design, argued that the chief obstruction in the way of building better houses was the superstition that they should be built in a style. There is a great difference between being built in an imitative style – Elizabethan, Jacobean, Georgian – and being built with style. A motorcar is built with thought for 'style' – that is, finish and elegance – but it is not built to look like a sedan chair or a stagecoach. To be concerned with style imitations and what the Americans call 'period design' is, he argued, not only irrational but also blocks the way to any possibility of true development.[37]

Walter Gropius thought that the beauty of automobiles should not depend on decorations or ornaments but rather on the harmony of the whole organism, on the logic of its function. He felt that the modern utilitarian car for everyday use should be technically perfect, beautiful and cheap.

In *The Modern House*, published in 1934, the architect FRS Yorke observed that once we become familiar with machines and standard machine products, we discover their balanced harmony, clear planes, exciting curves and powerful shapes. Yorke thought that there was no aesthetic law for the typical form of an industrial product; only one rule applied: if it gives perfect service, it is appropriate to its purpose. Its elegance comes from its smooth, perfect performance and from the qualities of the materials. Like other architects, Yorke used the example of the car as the machine most familiar to us when discussing the machine aesthetic and its effect on architectural design. He argued that the car grows more beautiful in form and line as it approaches mechanical perfection. Yorke also made the point that the car has achieved a standard of machine-beauty uncompromised by aesthetic prejudice. Thus, while architecture suffers because the public insists and expects it to be 'artistic', car design is not considered as art in the same sense and so is unhampered by sentiment or artistic titivation. At the same time, Yorke stressed that a house and an automobile are built for equally functional purposes.[38]

The Automobile as a Work of Art

In 1951, the architect Philip Johnson, Director of the Department of Architecture and Design at the Museum of Modern Art in New York, arranged the first exhibition of cars selected for the quality of their design. Called 'Eight Automobiles', it showed cars chosen for their excellence as works of art and for their relevance to contemporary problems of passenger car design. Displayed in the first-floor gallery and in the museum garden, the eight cars had varied designs: there was a 1930 Mercedes Model SS, Pininfarina's 1949 Cisitalia coupé, a Bentley and a three-seater Talbot both from 1939, a 1951 Jeep, a 1937 Cord, a Model TC MG from 1948, and a Lincoln Continental from 1941. Johnson said of the exhibition: 'An automobile is a familiar twentieth-century artefact, and is no less worthy of being judged for its visual appeal than a building or a chair. Automobiles are hollow, rolling sculpture, and the refinements of their design are fascinating. We have selected cars whose details and basic design suggest that automobiles, besides being America's most useful Useful Objects, could be a source

24

Cover of the 'Ten Automobiles' exhibition catalogue, The Museum of Modern Art, New York, 1953, showing the wheel 'hub cap' of Raymond Loewy's 1953 Studebaker Commander V-8 Starliner coupé.

exhibition **TEN AUTOMOBILES** *The Museum of Modern Art*

of visual experience more enjoyable than they now are.'[39]

Time magazine commented, tongue in cheek, that 'visitors to Manhattan's Museum of Modern Art have seen everything from eggbeaters to garbage cans displayed as works of art. Last week it was automobiles. On crushed stone runways in the museum's first-floor galleries stood shining examples of what the museum calls "hollow rolling sculpture".' *Time* continued, quoting the Curator of the Museum's Department of Architecture and Design, Arthur Drexler, who stated that the American Jeep had 'the combined appeal of an intelligent dog and a perfect gadget … [it] looks like a sturdy sardine can on wheels … [and is] one of the few genuine expressions of machine art.'

Undeterred, two years later, Drexler (still under the Directorship of Philip Johnson) organised another show, this time called 'Ten Automobiles'. A celebration of the Italian Cisitalia design, it included a display of cars that were all modelled in some way on that advanced automobile. This was a rather uniform selection of automobiles, all with similar fixed-head or fastback coupé bodies: a 1952 Cunningham Model C-4, a Lancia Grand Turismo from 1951, a 1950 Model DB2 Aston Martin, a 1953 Studebaker Commander V-8 Starliner coupé designed by Raymond Loewy, a French Ford Comete from 1952, a 1950 Simca Model 8 Sport, a Model TD MG from 1950, a 1952 Nash-Healey, a 1951 Siata Daina 1400, and a Porsche 1500 Super from 1952.

The reviews of this exhibition were less caustic but still betrayed a large degree of scepticism. The *New York Herald Tribune*'s critic Emily Genauer wrote: 'Admitting that "we do not require an automobile to reveal the spiritual insights characteristic of sculpture", the Museum of Modern Art still insists that the ten automobiles it is currently displaying in the marble-paved garden [redesigned in 1951-53 by Philip Johnson] where lately it showed sculpture by Rodin, Maillol and Epstein, are there because of "their excellence as works of art". Apparently works of art, according to the museum's definition, do not necessarily involve spiritual insights. Merely as a display of automobile design – not works of art, just as a group of ten new cars – the show is not only interesting but perhaps legitimately within the museum's territory, since it has long been dedicated to the improvement of industrial design … Some cars are highly impractical. The Porsche, for instance, has a fender, which is one piece with the whole back of the car. A bad dent and the repair job is phenomenally costly. The museum's curator of cars says this is no problem. People who buy Porsches throw them away when they get dented.'[40] The *New Yorker*'s correspondent, determined to have some fun, plagued Drexler with awkward questions during the press preview, later reporting that, 'Drexler took us up myrtle and down marble around the garden and called our attention to the fact that the Studebaker's hood [bonnet] is lower than the adjoining fenders. "Better visibility for the driver?" we asked, thinking old-fashioned, drive-yourself thoughts. "Greater refinement of design", said Drexler … We asked the price of the Cunningham and the Nash-Healey, and again we perceived we had put our foot in it. "I honestly don't know what any of these cars cost", Drexler said, his young face as long as the Simca he was standing by … "My own favourite car in this show is the Siata," Drexler said leading us to it … "Handle nicely, does it?" we asked and could have kicked ourselves. "I don't drive", said Drexler and by then his face was as long as a Lancia and getting longer.'[41]

The French painter André Derain would not have agreed with the critics, however. He insisted that his Bugatti was more beautiful than any work of art. Nor would the sculptor Henry Moore, who described automobiles as sculptures in motion and whose favourite car was the Jaguar Mark II. In 1930, the German writer Alfred Döblin proclaimed that the car dynamo was more beautiful than Cologne cathedral. Three years earlier, writer and playwright Lion Feuchtwanger had declared in one of his plays that when Gloria tyres were made, God's creation of the world had been completed. In 1902, another German writer, Otto Julius Bierbaum, author of *A Sentimental Journey by Automobile* (1903), made a three-month trip from Berlin across the Alps to Sorrento in an 865cc 8hp Adler. He wrote that the automobile must have enough self-confidence to look like a machine, and that it could be beautiful – not as beautiful as a horse, because only God can create such beauty, but at least as beautiful as an ocean liner.

The Swiss painter, sculptor and architect Max Bill, who studied at the Bauhaus and drove a 1947 Bentley Mark VI, wrote that designers who realise new forms are reacting, consciously or unconsciously, to trends in contemporary art, because it is in art that the intellectual and spiritual currents of every epoch find their viable expression. A comparison between automobiles and contemporary sculptures shows how close the relationship is between works of art and utilitarian forms.

The Italian Futurist artist Gino Severini wrote in 1922 that: 'there is an analogy between a machine and a work of art. For instance, all the various material components that go to make up an engine are directed by a single will – that of its inventor, which adds another kind of life, action or movement to the integral vitality of these various materials. The method used for constructing a machine is similar to that of constructing a work of art. If we also consider a machine from the point of view of the effect it creates on the beholder we will again discover that there is an analogy here with the work of art. In fact, unless you are completely blinded by some form of prejudice, you

Le Corbusier, proud owner of the luxury Voisin 10 CV, 1925. (Fondation Le Corbusier)

Le Corbusier driving on the roof test-track of the Lingotto plant, Turin, in a Fiat Balilla Sport 508S, 1934. (Fondation Le Corbusier)

View of Villa Stein-de-Monzie, Garches, 1927, with Le Corbusier's Voisin 10 CV deliberately positioned for a comparison of his architecture with an engineer-designed object. Ironically, Le Corbusier did not realise that his Voisin was designed by an architect and that he was actually comparing 'architecture' with architecture. (Fondation Le Corbusier)

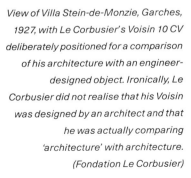

cannot fail to experience a feeling of pleasure, of admiration, when you are confronted by a well-built machine.'[42]

Indeed, some people are enthralled by particular automobile designs, collecting them as objects to be worshipped. Gio Ponti (the Italian architect who designed the Pirelli building in Milan between 1957 and 1960) and his partners Antonio Fornaroli and Alberto Rosselli each bought a Citroën DS19 when it went on sale in 1957, and in doing so paid homage to the beauty of the car and the genius of its designer, Flaminio Bertoni. Ponti loved his 'Goddess' and drove her whenever he could get away from his busy architectural schedule.

Although they would deny it vigorously, architects tend to be romantics at heart. In 1994, Norman Foster admitted, 'I enjoy more than most the romance and mobility that the car can offer.'[43] Part of architects' attraction to cars lies in the joy and pleasure of using the car and the satisfaction of handling a beautiful object. A number of photographs show Le Corbusier standing by his angular, 1925, 1.5-litre, four-cylinder, model C7, 10hp, two-door, Lumineuse-body Voisin (registration number 7316.X6).[44] Another photograph shows him at the wheel of the smart, 1934, Fiat Balilla Sport 508S, proudly trying it out on the test-track on the roof of the Lingotto assembly plant in Turin, which was designed by Giacomo Matté-Trucco between 1915 and 1921. (Apparently, Le Corbusier was trying to persuade Fiat to donate this car for the use of his office.) Later, he wrote a tribute to the Italian company saying that 'the time has come when we have to begin to build cities with the same confidence, the same courage, with the same spirit shown by the directors of Fiat. Beside that, there are many other things that the Fiat proposes and which are interesting for architecture and urbanism in the country.'[45]

It is not a Fiat, however, but Le Corbusier's 10hp Voisin that features in most photographs of his early buildings,[46] making a deliberate comparison between a machine for travel and a *machine à habiter*. Whole chapters of Le Corbusier's books are devoted to automobiles, ships, aeroplanes and other machines. In his 1925 Pavillon de l'Esprit nouveau, Le Corbusier showed furniture supported on tubular steel legs and frames, being most pleased with the staircase, which was constructed of bent and curved tubes: 'We have made a staircase like a bicycle chassis.'[47] Giving a lecture entitled 'The Undertaking of Furniture' during a visit to Buenos Aires in October 1929, he described his chaise longue as: 'the true machine for resting', explaining 'my weight alone was enough to keep it in the chosen position; no mechanism was needed.'

Like Le Corbusier, Frank Lloyd Wright was also enamoured with motorcars. Photographs show him seated at the wheel of his favourite convertibles, sporting all the right headgear. He loved large, powerful, ostentatious automobiles, especially open convertibles. Whether times were good or bad, he treated himself to the best models, owning during his lifetime a Stoddard-Dayton, a Knox, a Cord L29 and 810, a Cadillac, a Lincoln Zephyr, two Lincoln Continentals, a Packard, and other American, German and British makes. Wright's cars also included a fleet of Bantams in the late 1930s and Crosley Hotshot and Super Sports roadsters in the 1950s to transport his staff each autumn and spring between Taliesin at Spring Green, Wisconsin, and Taliesin West at Scottsdale, Arizona. He also admired the Citroën DS19, which he saw in Paris in 1956, although the car was not yet available for export.

Wright always tried to buy the newest models, characteristically negotiating a substantial discount with the

car dealers: 'You know it is a very valuable advertisement for your company if you publish in the newspapers that the famous Frank Lloyd Wright has bought the new Cord!'[48] Wright's persuasive approach paid off: he received a 50 per cent discount on the luxury front-wheel-drive 1929 Cord L29. Later, in 1936, he purchased another Cord – the 810 model with convertible body.

Machines for Living

Wright's views about the relationship between architecture and machines differed radically from Le Corbusier's, as the Czech architect Vladimír Karfík recalled in his memoir *Architekt si spomína (An Architect Remembers)*.[49] Karfík worked for Le Corbusier in Paris between 1925 and 1926, and in 1928-29 practised at Taliesin East and West with Frank Lloyd Wright. One day in 1928, while working for Wright, Karfík brought some architectural

Frank Lloyd Wright with the newly delivered red-and-black Mercedes-Benz 300 saloon, and a gull-wing 300 SL model ordered for Wesley Peters at Hillside School at Taliesin, Spring Green, Wisconsin, 1956. (The Frank Lloyd Wright Foundation)

magazines to the studio, which included articles by Le Corbusier. Wright showed great interest in the writings of his colleague but, when he had finished reading, he heaved a deep sigh and delivered a short lecture on Le Corbusier's misleading concepts of architecture. In Wright's view, the architect had to use machines, but machines must never be allowed to use the architect. Unlike Le Corbusier, who believed that a house is a machine for living, Wright defined his architecture as 'organic'. For him, 'organic' architecture was like a tree growing in a natural setting: you could cut off a branch and a new one would grow, even more beautiful; similarly, Wright's houses could be changed, extended or partly demolished – and yet stay alive. By contrast, argued Wright, with Le Corbusier's 'machinist' architecture the removal of one single little wheel would destroy it.

So while Le Corbusier maintained that his buildings were functionally and formally acceptable anywhere in the world, like a Ford automobile that can be driven with equal ease from India to Scandinavia, Wright found such statements totally unacceptable. For him, architecture had to grow from the soil and climate as naturally as trees. Machines, he felt, should be used in the new building technology, which may enrich architecture, but the 'humanistic' and 'organic' aspects must be more important than the 'machinery'.[50] It is therefore not surprising that to Le Corbusier's proclamation that a 'house is a machine for living in', Wright responded 'Yes, but only insofar as the human heart is a suction pump.' Yet both of them loved automobiles.

Peter Blake, the American architectural writer, explained the alleged absence of the human factor from Le Corbusier's view of the machine world by pointing out that he was talking about *French* machines – machines that were exquisitely beautiful but that did not necessarily work very well.[51] Le Corbusier saw them as poetic machines; his own machines and architecture were full of poetry, light and art as well as up-to-date technology.

Meanwhile, the architect and influential author Robert Venturi picked up the other contentious issue mentioned by Wright: the completeness and intactness of modern architecture. Venturi believes that 'the introduction of one foreign element [can] cast into doubt the entire effect of some modern buildings. Our buildings must survive the cigarette machine.'[52] Unlike untouchable architecture, machines have the ability to be repaired, altered, extended, enlarged or adapted for different uses; the modern machine architecture of the 1930s failed to learn this particular lesson.

In 1996 the Czech architect Jan Kaplicky, founder of the London-based avant-garde architectural practice Future Systems, published a small book called *For Inspiration Only.*[53] It is a collection of startling images and photographs assembled to show everyday objects and natural shapes suggesting new forms. Among these images are more than a dozen of automobiles and their parts, and more than two dozen of aircraft, boats and spacecraft. Kaplicky's book indicates how crucial it is for designers to keep up to date with progress in technology and other design disciplines and to be constantly alert to the world around us.

Architects as Designers of Automotive Objects

Moving on from the cultural assimilation of the motor car and its implications for architecture, this chapter presents a chronological survey of architects who have been involved with automotive design. This involvement ranges from hypothetical schemes that went no further than the architect's sketchbooks to commissions from individuals or companies to bring innovation, new approaches and fresh ideas to the automobile industry. Acquaintance with their designs provides an insight into their lives and work, and inspiration for future endeavours.

Joseph Aloysius Hansom

Hansom (1803-82) was an architect and editor of *The Builder* magazine. He became interested in horse-driven vehicles and in particular the coaches used for hire as Hackney cabs. In 1834, he designed a large vehicle carried on a pair of wheels, which were 7 feet 6 inches in diameter and which had their short axles located in the centre of the body to enable passengers to enter the cab easily via the nearside door. The driver was positioned high up at the front of the body. This arrangement made the whole cab very stable. Subsequently, smaller diameter wheels were fitted and the driver's seat was moved to the front of the roof. Thereafter, the wheels were fixed to a cranked axle; windows were placed in the sides and a pair of half doors at the front afforded protection to passengers. The driver was moved again, this time to the rear of the cab, high enough up for him to see the road in front of the horse's head. Hansom's cab became a popular form of transport and its use spread to most cities of the world.

A widely read book published in 1886 helped to celebrate the Hansom cab, making it even more popular. Written by a young Australian barrister's clerk Fergus Hume *The Mystery of a Hansom Cab* was inspired by a late-night journey to St Kilda, a suburb of Melbourne. It told the story of a cabby who discovers to his horror that his drunken passenger has been mysteriously poisoned with a chloroform-saturated handkerchief.

Left: the original Hansom cab design of 1834; centre: the Hackney carriage, which preceded it; right: John Chapman's improved Hansom cab. (Illustrated London News)

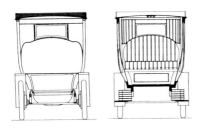

Josef Maria Olbrich: design for Opel, 1906, side and rear elevations and cross section. The proposal did not differ from the mainstream notion of vehicle body forms of that time. (Staatliche Museen zu Berlin, Kunstbibliothek)

Joseph Maria Olbrich

In 1886, in Rösselsheim, Germany, the sewing-machine manufacturers, the Opel brothers began to make bicycles and then motorcars. At first, Opel based its car production on a model developed by Friedrich Lutzmann, whose company it took over in 1898. This car was, however, rather primitive and out of date, and only thirty-five were sold in two years before Opel ceased production. The following year, the Opel brothers decided to persist with motorcar manufacture and imported a number of small, single-cylinder engine chassis from the French company Darracq, which they fitted with their own bodies. This model sold well and, starting in 1902, new twin- and four-cylinder Opels of various body designs were developed. The connection with Darracq was discontinued in 1906 and from then on, only cars wholly designed by Opel were made. Production increased, and between the beginning of 1902 and the end of 1906 1,370 cars left the Opel factory. In 1903 Opel began racing its cars, gathering trophies from various competitions.

The Austrian architect Josef Maria Olbrich (1867-1908) remodelled a car for Opel while designing a worker's family house for the company at Mathildenhöhe in Darmstadt (1907-08). Sketches drawn in 1906 show a rear elevation, an interior section, and a side view and perspective view of a coupé de ville body. The car's design does not differ greatly from the models being produced by Opel at the time, though the striped interior combined with curved elements carries echoes of the Viennese Secession (of which Olbrich was a co-founder) and Werkstätte styles. The design was never realised and may simply have been a theoretical exercise .

Frank Lloyd Wright

Wright (1867-1959) was one of the most prolific architect-car designers. His first car was a 1910 Stoddard-Dayton roadster. His son , John Wright, remembers in his book *My Father Who is on Earth* how excitement ran high on the day the four-cylinder, three-seater car arrived. 'It was one of three automobiles in all of Oak Park. Dad had the factory remake the original body according to his design. There were two individual seats in front, one directly centred behind ... A cantilever convertible canvas top streamlined from the back to well in front of the dashboard. The trimmings were brass, the body enamelled a straw yellow ... The good citizens of Oak Park called it the Yellow Devil, and not many days passed before the Oak Park police threatened to confiscate it. The speed law was 25 miles per hour. The Yellow Devil could go 60.'[54]

In his autobiography, Wright himself describes owning an Auburn Cord and some five other top makes. Usually unable to afford to buy the cars for cash, he paid for them by taking out instalment-plan contracts (hire-purchase agreements), which plagued him financially for years afterwards. Between 1922 and 1924, he drove a long, black, low, streamlined, specially built Cadillac with a patent leather Victoria hood over the rear seat. However, he preferred the Cord, 'a prideful car', which incorporated 'innovation along right lines', its design based on the principle of pulling with the front wheels. It had the best body design 'from my streamline standpoint' and in terms of 'it looking becoming to my houses.'[55]

Another favourite was Wright's Lincoln Continental. The car came about when Edsel Ford, the talented son of

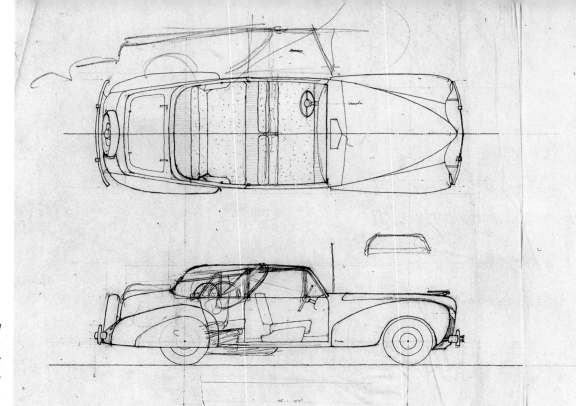

*Frank Lloyd Wright: remodelled
Lincoln Continental Cabriolet, 1940,
sketches and photograph. Wright
claimed that with this car he
influenced Raymond Loewy's ideas.
(The Frank Lloyd Wright Foundation)*

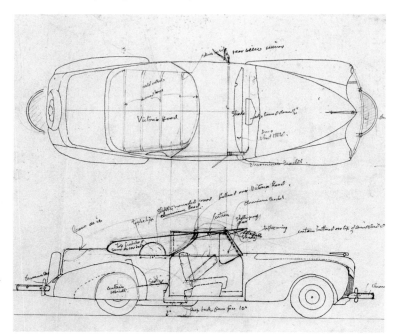

Henry Ford, used the rear-engined, aerodynamically styled Briggs Dream Car designed by John Tjaarda as a model for a new V12 Lincoln Zephyr, launched in 1936. In 1938, Edsel decided to produce a custom-built luxury car and, using the Zephyr chassis, proposed a special, low, convertible body, which was completed in February 1939. Limited production followed the next year, and the car was named the Lincoln Continental. becoming one of the most admired American designs. Edsel arranged a private sale, sending invitations adorned with a beautiful drawing of the car to prominent people. Wright loved it, and decided to buy the Continental Cabriolet even though he could not afford it.

Eugene Masselink, Wright's assistant, describes their arrival at the Lincoln showroom to purchase the 1940 Cabriolet: 'Mr Wright swept into the agency and started thumping the tyres with his hickory staff. This was no ordinary day in the Lincoln agency. This was the day the first Lincoln Continentals appeared on the showroom floors ... A salesman glided over to us. Mr Wright waved his staff: "I'll take this one ..." He tapped the convertible's top. "And paint it Cherokee red! Gene here will give you a colour swatch." Mr Wright turned and marched out the door. The salesman stood there frozen, mouth open, while Gene found the swatch. "It's all right" Gene told the man. "Mr Wright knows Edsel Ford".'[56]

Apart from his earliest automobiles, all Wright's cars were painted Cherokee red, a colour inspired by a small pottery vase he greatly admired. 'The colour red is invincible. It is the colour not only of the blood – it is the colour of creation. It is the only life-giving colour in nature filling the sprouting plant with life and giving warmth to everything in creation.'[57]

After the Lincoln overturned in an accident while being driven by Wright's son-in-law William Wesley Peters, Wright made several sketches proposing to modify the body. He lowered the front soft-leather roof and reduced the windscreen by five inches. In this modified design, the rear roof section was in metal and was taller than the original, while the back window was omitted. The back seat was set further down and – since Wright liked his privacy – a pair of leather curtains separated the driver from the back. The most radical changes were to the rear side windows, which became semicircular. They were explained as frames to the architect's vista – the horizon line with a sky hemisphere above.

Wright later claimed that Raymond Loewy used his changes to the Lincoln as inspiration when in 1945 he modified two Continentals, one for himself and one for a friend. Loewy integrated the rear portion of the boot, wings and pavilion into one flowing form, but for the front roof portion he used a hard Lucite top. The side windows were circular portholes filled with blue glass.

In 1941, Wright purchased another Lincoln Continental, this time a coupé. Though he carried out only minor exterior modifications to it, the whole interior was redone in Cherokee red to match the exterior colour at the cost of $2,000. The two Lincoln Continentals proved to be Wright's favourite cars, and he kept both of them until his death.

During his lifetime, Wright drove the equivalent of more than seven times around the globe without a single accident or 'even a smashed fender' until he collided with a florist's truck in the 1930s. At that point, he gave up

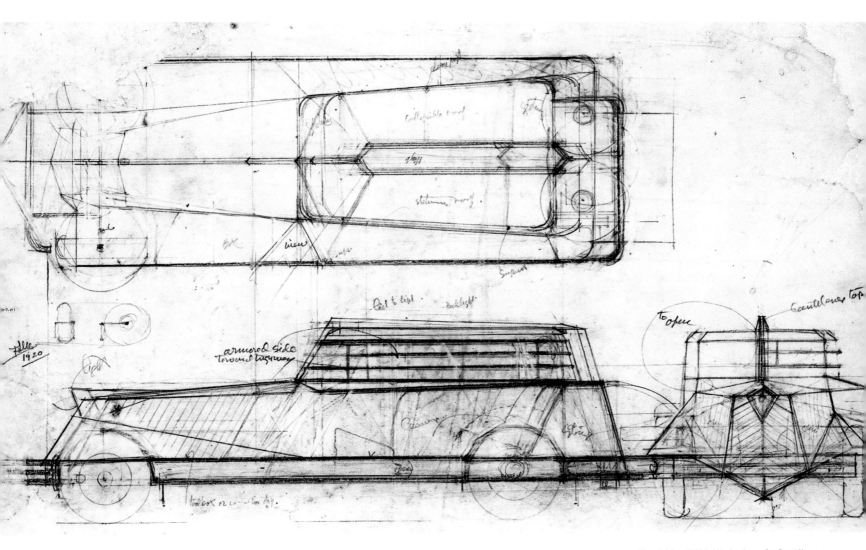

Frank Lloyd Wright: design of a Cantilever car, 1920. It displays unusual treatment of the driver's windscreen. The roof is suspended from an illuminated central cantilever beam. (The Frank Lloyd Wright Foundation)

driving, but even then would urge his chauffeur to overtake whenever there was a car in front. If his driver did not obey, Wright would become angry, shouting 'go fast, but don't speed!' Looking back on his job as Wright's driver, Richard Carney remarked: 'Once when I drove him from Madison to Spring Green, he insisted that I never go below 100 miles per hour. It was the most horrifying drive. But Mr Wright was pleased.'[58]

Ironically, Wright despised most American automobile designs of the time. saying that the only mobile thing about the American automobile was its name. The cars had good engines but the designs were bad. They looked as though they were made to fight each other in the street. Mobility argued Wright, should be like a school of fish, all working together. The American automobile, he felt, lacked that quality.

After redesigning his own Stoddard-Dayton, by 1920 he had already produced a sketch for an unusual car body with a cantilevered top. Plan, side and front elevations exist in the Wright archives. The car roof was suspended from a central beam, which appeared to be backlit and covered in glass. The passenger part of the roof was openable along the beam but the chauffeur's side was fixed. The windscreen was armoured towards the highway. Unusually, both the windscreen and the side windows were shaded with brise-soleil louvres on the driver's side only. The proposed chassis was made out of a box platform and the car was given a streamlined look by its back-sloping radiator. The headlights moved with the steering.

Wright thought about the perfect car design over a number of years and in 1955 he started to sketch an idea he called the 'Road Machine.' The proposal was based on an International Harvester Tractor M used on his Wisconsin farm. The Road Machine was meant to be a three-seater taxi with a wheelbase 15 feet long. The engine directly drove two large centre wheels with one front wheel and one rear wheel. Like the driver of the Hansom cab, that of the Road Machine, steering with a tiller, sat high above the passengers in his own compartment, with a clear view of the road ahead. A 1958 sketch modifies this design by repositioning the large stainless-steel spoked wheels and the engine to the rear, using two wheels close together at the front, and providing four passenger seats as well as the driver's seat high up. A refinement of the first idea of a three-seater can be seen in another sketch from 1958. This proposal was intended as part of Broadacre City, Wright's Utopian dream of a close-to-nature environment for a society engaged in pleasure, leisure and the pursuit of the arts. Wright explored other forms of transport in Broadacre City, including a cylinder-shaped, propeller-driven train riding on a monorail or ball bearings (1958) and a helicopter (1959), which was later altered to a flying-saucer-like machine.

Adolf Loos

Adolf Loos, (1870-1933) a truly Central European architect, was born in Brno, Moravia, now part of the Czech Republic, but he lived most of his life in Vienna. He spent three years in the United States, later visiting London and Paris. In 1908 he published his essay 'Ornament und Verbrechen', in which he spoke out against the use of ornament in modern architecture and arts and crafts. In his plain, cubic houses and villas he employed his idea of volumetric planning (*Raumplan*), in which individual spaces were placed on different levels and yet were

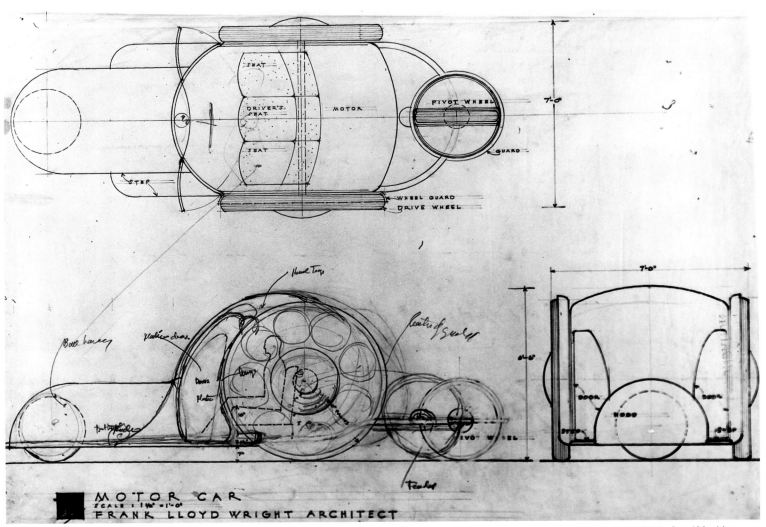

MOTOR CAR
SCALE : 1½" = 1'-0"
FRANK LLOYD WRIGHT ARCHITECT

Frank Lloyd Wright: Road Machine proposals, 1955 and 1958. The form is reminiscent of a Hansom cab. (The Frank Lloyd Wright Foundation)

ROAD
MACHINE

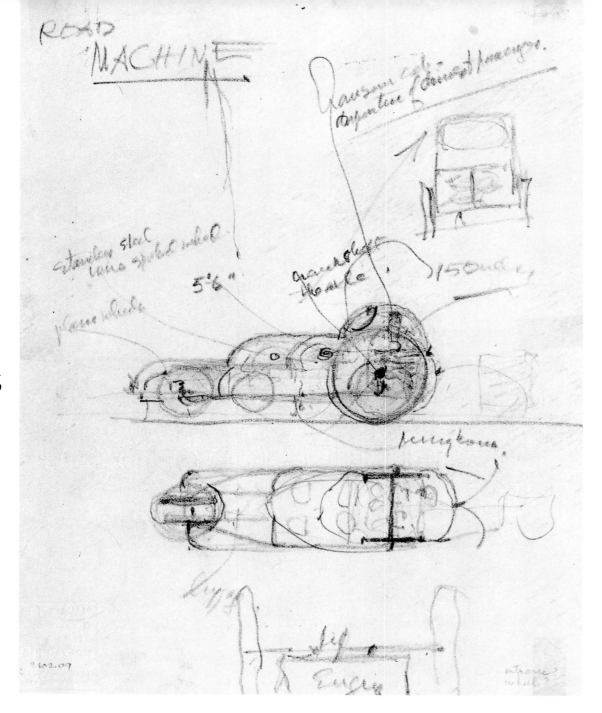

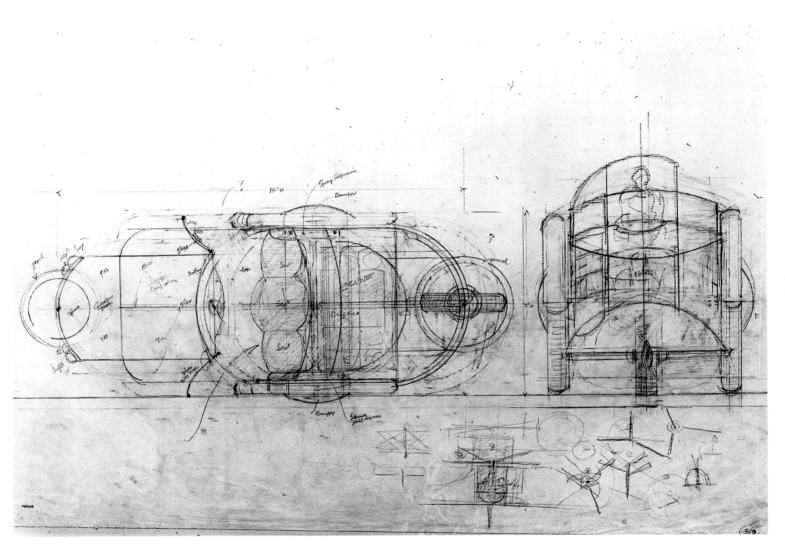

interwoven, creating a complex but compact whole.

The Loos archives contain two pieces of paper covered with studies for car designs. One is drawn on a rent reminder from a Parisian landlord, the other on an envelope addressed to 'Adolphe Loos'. Dating from 1923, these drawings show a proposal for Lancia. What inspired Loos to propose a car for this particular manufacturer? We can only suppose that it was because he was captivated by the revolutionary Lancia Lambda, produced a year earlier.

The Lambda was the creation of Vincenzo Lancia, who started his career as a test driver at Fiat and in 1900 became the company's driver, participating in a number of races with great success. At the end of 1906, Lancia founded his own car manufacturing company, Lancia & Cia Fabrica Automobili. By September 1907, the first 12hp Lancia was being tested and Lancia's legend of excellence had begun. Late in 1918, Lancia applied for a patent for the first genuine monocoque body structure (though similar attempts at producing a monocoque structure had already been made) and, inspired by the stiff, steel structure of a ship's hull, produced a car body design. This was to become the Lambda prototype, which was ready for testing on the Italian roads in September 1921. When the car went into production, the complete hull concept was altered to a 2-millimetre-thick, pressed-

Adolf Loos: sketches for the Lancia, on an envelope and a rent reminder, 1923. (Adolf Loos Archiv, Albertina Museum, Wien)

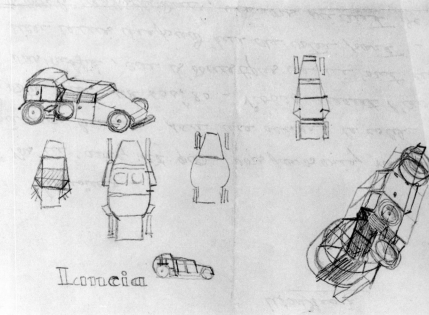

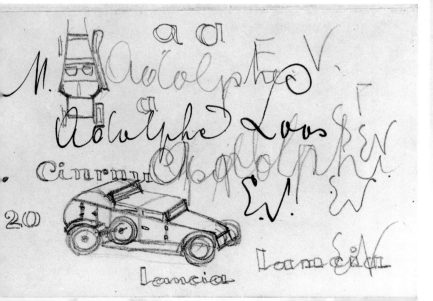

Walter Gropius: Adler Favorit cabriolet, 1930. Two body versions built by Wilhelm Karmann of Osnabrück. (Bauhaus-Archiv, Berlin)

steel skeleton to reduce the bodyweight while maintaining the strength and torsional rigidity. The Lambda was an immediate success and Lancia became known as one of the most progressive manufacturers of the early 1920s.

In his sketches, Loos endeavoured to introduce new ideas into car body form. His aim was the optimum use of space. The sketches indicate that there could possibly be three rows of seats. To enable passengers to see forward, the rear of the car is raised above the front. From the bonnet to the rear the body rises three levels. The end of the car is curved behind the rear axle and in this way, the body achieves an overall streamlined form. In plan, the width of the car body is enlarged to the maximum between the axles to gain ideal comfort for the passengers. This was a new notion at a time when all cars had straight running boards stretching from the front to the rear wing. For ease and low cost of manufacture, most of the body panels in Loos' design were flat and rectangular. The proposal was ahead of its time and highly individual.

Indeed Loos' thinking was always ahead of its time. In 1925, while still living in Paris, designing and overseeing the construction of Tristan Tzara's house, he mentioned to the Czech architect Vladimír Karfík that good architecture could be described, not necessarily drawn. Words, however, were not the only way to express volumes in space. Mathematics could do the same. Every point in space could be established by three geometrical co-ordinates and in this way a good project could be described mathematically. Loos added that he could imagine himself sitting in an armchair, dictating a project to his assistant in only words and numbers. It would, he believed, be necessary to invent various machines to replace primitive set-squares and tee-squares.[59] Seventy years later, computers are used in all aspects of architectural design and construction.

Walter Gropius

A German architect, industrial designer and teacher, Gropius (1883-1969) was director of the Bauhaus at Weimar and Dessau in Germany from 1919 to 1928. He was also, between 1929 and 1933, chairman of the committee for body design at the Adler-Automobilwerke in Frankfurt-am-Main. During this time at Adler, Gropius proposed six types of car body for luxury limousines and cabriolets, and one of each was constructed.

Gropius was a friend of the Kleyer family, owners of Adler. Heinrich Kleyer, the company founder, had initially established a bicycle factory in Frankfurt in 1880 after witnessing a cycle race during a visit to New York. To begin with, Kleyer imported bicycles, which he marketed under the name of Herold, but as sales increased he started his own manufacture. Soon, he was building a new six-storey headquarters, at the time the tallest industrial structure in Frankfurt. The top floor was used for bicycle-testing and instructing new owners. Kleyer changed the name of his bicycles to Adler (German for 'eagle') to imply flight and also to gain the first place in any alphabetical listing. In 1898, Kleyer obtained the licence to make DeDion cars, producing the first Adler automobile two years later. Among the designers employed by Adler as motorcar production increased was Edmund Rumpler, who proposed various two- and four-cylinder engines. With this standard of technical design back-up, Adler cars performed well in long-distance rallies and trials. As demand for Adler cars grew, so did the range of models

Walter Gropius: Adler Standard 6 cabriolet, 1931, view of the interior. (Bauhaus-Archiv, Berlin)

Walter Gropius: Adler Standard 6 cabriolet, 1931. One of the first cars with an arrangement of seats that fold down into sleeping couchettes. It could be assumed that by providing the sleeping accommodation, Gropius envisaged a car as a house on wheels, which is why his automobile designs were stilted, lacking the necessary expression of mobility. (Bauhaus-Archiv, Berlin)

Walter Gropius: Adler Standard 6, 1931, rear view. (Bauhaus-Archiv, Berlin)

Walter Gropius: Adler Standard 8 limousine, 1931. Some opinions assert that employing Gropius was a marketing ploy aimed at attracting publicity to technically outdated products. On all Adler designs, Gropius co-operated with engineer M Rachlis, scuptor D Paulon and Professor R Lisker. (Adlerwerke, H Kleyer AG)

Walter Gropius: Adler Standard 6,
cabriolet, 1931 with perforated radiator
grille. Ise Gropius standing beside the car.
(Bauhaus-Archiv, Berlin)

available. By the end of 1926, the company employed a 6,000-strong workforce and had captured 10 per cent of the German market.

The first Gropius design to be realised for Adler was the 1930 Favorit cabriolet, followed by the 1931 Standard 6 cabriolet. The Standard 6 design did not differ greatly from contemporary production – the body emphasis was on extended verticality and a total absence of horizontal lines. However, the interior seating was interestingly arranged so that the front and back seats could be joined into sleeping couchettes by lowering the backrests of the front seats. Highly polished full-wheel discs – very unusual in Germany at the time – were fitted. A stylised chrome version of the Adler eagle mascot was fixed over a perforated, or finned, chromed radiator grille. The colour scheme, including that of the interior, was restrained to give a discreet impression. The other two Gropius-designed Adler bodies were for the four- to five-seater, 2.6-litre, 50hp, Adler Standard 6 limousine and the large six- to seven-seater, 80hp, Adler Standard 8 Pullman limousine. All coachwork for the Standard prototypes was made by Josef Neuss of Berlin.

Opinions about the Gropius designs for Adler varied greatly. The cabriolet was especially acclaimed in several reviews and was even used in a theatre play in which the couchettes provided a contemporary situation for a lovers' encounter. In general, however, it was assumed that Gropius' design work for Adler was a formal experiment that would have little influence on the future development of car design. Though elegant and 'classical', with their vertical rectangular emphasis, Gropius' automobile designs betrayed his background as someone more used to the design of static objects. They lacked the dynamic quality and symbolic expression of movement that are necessarily bound into the concept of the automobile.

Walter Gropius: diesel railcar manufactured by Waggonfabrik L Steinfurth of Königsberg for Prussian State Railway Carriage Company, 1913. (Bauhaus-Archiv, Berlin)

Earlier, in 1913, Gropius had designed a diesel railcar, which had been commissioned by the Prussian State Railway Carriage Company in Königsberg. The engine and driver's compartment followed pure functionalist principles. The cylinders were in line along the raised centre of the car; the elevated front of the car, which housed the engine, was extended in a streamlined form to the exhaust pipe, terminating at roof level, while the lower side sections allowed a good view from the driver's cabin. The front part of the car body could slide forwards to give access to the engine for maintenance. This design was ahead of its time and, according to Gropius, the client was very satisfied with the car because the hot air from the engine was smoothly expelled under the slanting nose.

Pierre-Jules Boulanger

'Build a car for two farmers dressed for work, carrying along either 50 kilograms of potatoes or a small barrel of wine, an umbrella on four wheels.' This was Boulanger's brief to Maurice Broglie, his chief engineer at the Citroën works at Quai de Javel, Paris. Further requirements were for maximum comfort, a top speed of 60kph, a fuel consumption of three litres per 100 kilometres and a weight of 300 kilograms, all for one third of the retail price of the 7CV Traction Avant. Boulanger (1886-1950) had gained an understanding of the kind of thing that was required when working as the company architect for Michelin et Cie at Clermont-Ferrand in rural central France in the 1920s, designing low-cost housing for the factory workers.

A man of great technical capabilities and design vision, his central philosophy was that a car should be designed around driver and passenger requirements. After completing his national service flying aeroplanes and air balloons in the French Observer Corps, he travelled to the United States. There, he worked on a ranch, as a tram driver and finally as a draughtsman with a Seattle firm of architects. Later he moved to Canada to found his own design-and-build company. At the beginning of the First World War, he returned to France to enlist in the Armée de l'Air where he reached the rank of captain.

It was during the War that he got to know the Michelin brothers who, in 1918, invited him to design factory buildings for them in Clermont-Ferrand. He spent the next sixteen years at Michelin, until 1935, when André Citroën died, having failed to rescue his company from bankruptcy. Michelin, which had supplied Citroën with wheels and tyres ever since Citroën car manufacture started in 1919, took over the company and Boulanger was asked to take charge of the running of the factory in Paris.

Boulanger assembled a group of talented engineers and designers to realise his dream of a small, flexible, maintenance-free car, affordable by the population of the French countryside. The new project was called TPV ('Toute Petite Voiture'). André Lefébvre headed the team. He had worked for the aviation company Sup-Aéro and had subsequently designed and raced Voisin cars. After 1931 he worked briefly for Renault and in 1933 joined Citroën, designing the very successful 7CV and 11CV Traction Avant with the young Italian sculptor Flaminio Bertoni. Bertoni and Jean Muratet were appointed to develop the TPV body while Alphonse Forceau was responsible for the gearbox and suspension. Plans were made for a front-wheel-drive, platform-chassis-type car with easily removable body panels. Power was initially provided by an adapted, water-cooled, horizontally opposed, twin-cylinder 500cc BMW motorcycle engine. A wooden mock-up was made in 1936 and the first prototype followed a year later. Because both Boulanger and Lefébvre had experience of aircraft technology, the new car borrowed a number of lightweight aviation details and ideas: aluminium sheets were used for the body panels and platform construction while windows were made of mica; the simple cloth and tubular-frame seats were suspended via cables from the roof frame; the frame and support members were perforated; and the corrugation of the body panels was borrowed from the all-metal Junkers aeroplanes; the suspension was coped with torsion bars located under the rear seat.

Prototypes continued to be developed throughout 1937, all of them tested in secret to keep potential competitors such as Renault and other foreign companies at bay. The motorcycle engine did not work very efficiently and the later prototypes were fitted with a water-cooled, 375cc, flat-twin engine designed by Maurice Sainturat, the man responsible for the Traction Avant power unit.

Prototype testing proved that aluminium was not the right material for the job. It was costly and difficult to

Pierre-Jules Boulanger: 1939 Citroën 2CV, fully restored. (Citroën)

obtain; the body panels were hard to weld and the platform chassis, which had its frame members perforated to reduce weight, was too flexible. Details such as access for oil changes and the driver's field of vision also needed improving. There were other flaws: there was no rear-view mirror; the single front headlight, though legal at the time, was confusing for other motorists because it made the car look like a motorcycle in the dark, and the mica widows easily scratched. In May 1939, the Levallois factory was ordered to produce 250 cars, but only a handful was completed before the outbreak of the Second World War.

During the war, these completed examples were hidden, and the remaining prototypes and half-completed cars were supposedly destroyed. With Jean Cadiou, who now headed the TPV team, Boulanger decided to use the stronger steel rather than the light aluminium. Walter Becchia, who came from Talbot, redesigned the gearbox, adding a fourth overdrive gear and altering the 375cc engine to an air-cooled unit because of cold-start problems and the need for extra space for a radiator. The prime factor in the design was not to skimp on the technical aspects or the quality of the mechanical parts: the horizontally opposed twin engine was very efficient and simple, but it was expensively constructed in aluminium alloy with cylinder liners. It consisted of one-piece connecting rods and a built-up crankshaft. Primarily, the engine was handmade with extremely accurate machining on the facing surfaces, eliminating the usually troublesome head gaskets. The final suspension design consisted of four independently sprung wheels with inertia dampers incorporated into each. They were mounted on two front-leading arms and two rear-trailing arms. The arms were fixed to the platform frame by conical roller bearings and were connected to rods fitted to two interconnected longitudinal springs on each side. The overall design counterbalanced the expensive and complex engine and suspension with a minimalist but perfectly adequate interior. This brilliant design achieved a comfortable and effortless ride with minimum maintenance. The design team achieved almost all the goals they had set themselves except for one: the weight, which with the use of steel and other improvements climbed from the planned 300 kilograms to 495 kilograms including five litres of fuel. On this basis, production was approved early in 1948 on condition that the finished cars would be available for the autumn Paris Salon. The only body colour offered was a cool grey.

On 7 October 1948, the 35th Salon de l'Automobile was officially opened and the President of the French Republic, Vincent Auriol, was asked to present the new Citroën Deux Chevaux Vapeur. The cost of the new car was quoted as f185,000, rising in 1949 when the car went on the market for f228,000. The crowds and press were amazed and excited. It became immediately apparent that the Deux Chevaux would have a universal appeal, its unique personality and modern concept fitting exactly into the contemporary era. Soon the waiting period for delivery grew to two years. The legend was born. The 2CV became an essential feature of French life and society.

Having triumphantly concluded this project, Boulanger, Lefébvre and Bertoni proceeded with the next one, named the Voiture de Grande Diffusion (VGD), which was to be a successor to the Traction Avant. Some ideas had already been developed in 1945 and a long conception period, similar to that of the 2CV's was repeated. The result was the beautiful Citroën DS19, 'the Goddess', seen by the public for the first time in 1955. Unfortunately, the development of this car cost Boulanger his life – he died while testing one of the prototypes.

Pierre-Jules Boulanger: three, recently discovered
2CVs, from the 250 pre-production series of 1939,
found in a barn at Citroën's secret La Ferté Vidame
test centre. All three have water-cooled, 375cc,
flat-twin engines. (Citroën)

Boulanger showing off the first post-war production 2CV at the Paris Salon de l'Automobile, 1948. (Citroën)

Flaminio Bertoni: early study for the DS19 body form inspired by the initial Lefébvre's teardrop concept and one of the first finalised drawings from late 1954. In January 1955, the roof-line profile was raised to provide more headroom just prior to the first pre-production manufacture. (Citroën)

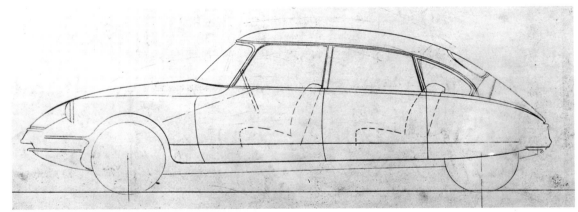

Le Corbusier (Charles-Edouard Jeanneret)

Le Corbusier (1887-1965) was born in the clock- and watch-making town of La Chaux-de-Fonds in the Swiss canton of Neuchâtel. Brought up surrounded by people making precision machines, it is perhaps natural that for him, machines became a symbol, an expression of human endeavour and an essential element of human existence. His view of the world was measured against the performance of machines and their ability, with human beings, to conquer all obstacles and bring solutions to the living world.

Le Corbusier admired automobiles, aircraft and ocean liners. His own car, a 1925, 10hp Voisin displaying the enormous 23-centimetre-high La Cocotte mascot, provided a standard for his buildings. Here was a design that fulfilled all of his five points of architecture: the Voisin was raised above the ground on wheels (*pilotis*), the body had a simple plan, a horizontal band of windows, a free façade and a flat roof. This is not surprising perhaps, since the Voisin's Lumineuse body had been designed by an architect, André Noël Noël-Telmont, who was in charge of the Voisin body shop between 1919 and 1936.

Indeed, in his 1955 article 'Machine Aesthetics', Reyner Banham pointed out that Le Corbusier unwittingly sabotaged his argument in praise of the quality of engineer-designed objects such as cars, as opposed to poor contemporary architectural standards because the designers and engineers he most admired had come from an art or architectural background: Gabriel Voisin was an architectural student, and Ettore Bugatti, André and Edouard Michelin, and aeroplane-designer Henry Farman were all art students before they embarked on their engineering careers.[60] These people all designed beautiful cars, aeroplanes and automobile accessories, which challenged the notion that pure engineering had created its own kind of beauty.

Le Corbusier's connection with Voisin began in the mid-1920s when he was seeking sponsorship for his architectural and urban designs. He had discussions with Peugeot, Citroën and Voisin, finally negotiating a deal with Voisin's administrative and financial director Eugène Mongermon and Bordeaux industrialist Henri Frugés. Mongermon and Frugés agreed to finance both the building of Le Corbusier's Pavillon de l'Esprit nouveau on the Cours de la Reine and the Plan of Paris for the 1925 Paris Exposition Internationale des Arts Décoratifs. The Plan of Paris, shown in the Pavilion, was named the Plan Voisin. The Plan was based on the idea that '*l'automobile a tué la grande ville; l'automobile doit sauver la grande ville*' ('the car has killed the city; the car must save the city'). This was a rather controversial notion – and the reason for other car manufacturers' refusal to add their names to the project.

Around this time, in March 1925, Le Corbusier obtained his 10hp Voisin car. It was a second-hand model and Mongermon gave f8,000 towards its cost in payment of Le Corbusier's fees for designing a house for him on a plot next to Villa La Roche-Jeanneret in Auteuil, Paris[61] (a new 10hp Voisin would have cost f67,500 in 1925, a second-hand model f50,000). The Voisin car expressed luxury and comfort and represented the successful, exclusive, élite way of life of the rich and famous members of the French upper classes. Voisin cars were owned by royalty, politicians, show-business people and sportsmen, and they were successful on the racing circuits. For Le Corbusier, the Voisin connection helped open the door to influential French high society and elevated his

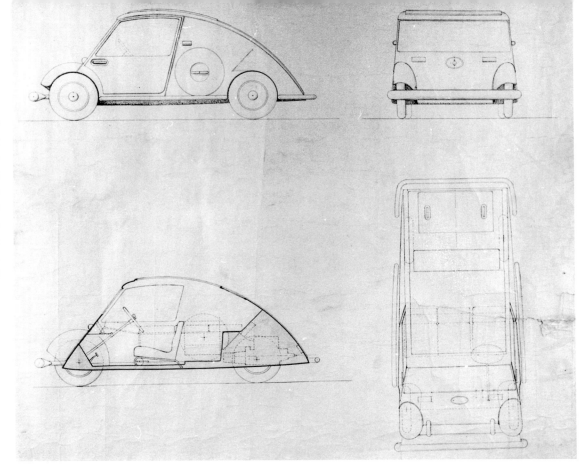

Le Corbusier and Pierre Jeanneret:
Voiture minimum, design development
sketches, 1928-36. The design
developed even beyond the
submission date for the SIA
competition held in 1935. The only
drawing in the whole series with a date
(31/1/36) indicates seating and a
possible sleeping position.
(Fondation Le Corbusier)

architecture to the same platform as his exclusive modern automobile.

According to his friends, Le Corbusier drove his Voisin rather recklessly. The Czech architect Karel Honzík visited Le Corbusier's atelier at 35 Rue de Sèvres in Paris in 1935. Afterwards, Le Corbusier drove Honzík and his wife to his new flat in the Porte Molitor apartment block. 'The Voisin car, into which we sat down as passengers and Le Corbusier drove, showed great signs of wear. The paint was cracked and almost faded. The windows were broken, fragments of glass tinkled under our soles. Our host kept clamped in his lips his everlasting cigarette made out of lethal naval tobacco. From the corner of his mouth Le Corbusier dropped a few words about a small car accident, which he had suffered a week before. He then warned us not to be alarmed by sudden jolting of the car, as he had to change gear directly from the first into third because the second gear was "stripped". Really the journey was rather unnerving because of the irregular noises, the horrific screeching of the first gear and the grating of the gearbox. It all sounded like a clamorous "rodeo" in the middle of busy boulevard junctions where hundreds of vehicles were constantly moving. It was obvious that Le Corbusier did not attach great significance to "small" technical defects. As regards the cult of machine, which he proclaimed, there was

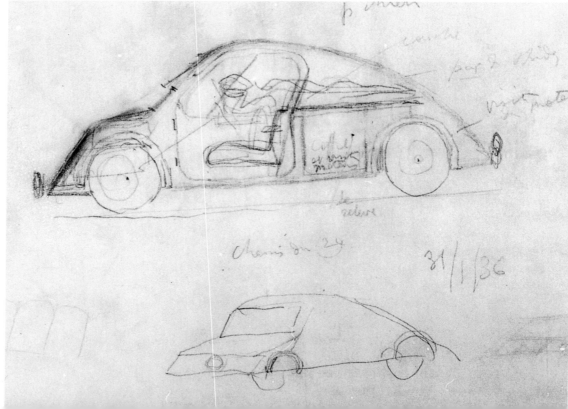

something inconsistent in his overlooking the faulty functions of his car.'[62]

By his own admission, Le Corbusier's early architecture and furniture designs were machines. His chapel at Ronchamp even looks like a spaceship that has landed on top of a hill; his houses – Maison Cook, Villa Savoye, Villa Stein-de-Monzie – are reminiscent of parts of Farman Goliath planes or the rear deck of Cunard's *Aquitania*. Le Corbusier confessed in *L'Esprit nouveau* no. 8 that he had chosen the stern of the *Aquitania* as an exemplary model for 'a villa located on the dunes of Normandy'. This was not a chance choice since the Cunard liner, built in 1913, is perceived in the history of shipbuilding as the paramount architectural achievement and final phase of the development of turbine-powered, four-funnel ships. Similarly Le Corbusier's *Unité d'habitation* projects in Marseilles, Nantes-Rezé, Briey, Firmini and Berlin were inspired by the organisational principle of the decks of the large ocean liners.

Le Corbusier implied a direct connection between the form and structure of the modern machine and the new architectural aesthetics. Villa Savoye is a good example. The ground floor is set in to allow a car to circulate under the building. The assumed motion of the car is continued by a ramp, which leads from the drop-off at ground level to the roof garden, with views of the landscape like a 'framed view through the car window that began the sequence. With the Villa Savoye the machine fully enters the garden. Through the architectural promenade, man and machine have become one.'[63]

It is interesting that Le Corbusier's smooth transformation of naval and aircraft architecture into building concepts was similarly applied, though in a reverse order, when he decided to design his Voiture minimum (sometimes termed 'maximum') in 1928. He went about the first proposals for the rear-engined car like an architect: in a plan form, then he drew elevations and sections and only later produced several perspective sketches.[64] The end result, which he and his cousin Pierre Jeanneret (with whom he then worked) submitted for the Société des Ingénieurs de l'Automobile (SIA) competition in 1935, was certainly innovative in its concept. However, it is seen as the solution for a simple building problem rather than a proposal for a complex, moving, dynamic object. The design of the car body was, surprisingly, very two-dimensional. No body or chassis structure was shown, nor any means of suspension. This indicates a superficial approach rather than a real understanding of essential car mechanics and structure. The final body design was wide and short in plan with three seats at the front, a transversal seat in the middle, and the rear section used for luggage, a spare tyre and the engine. The seats could be arranged into sleeping couchettes. The front and rear bumpers had tubular profiles with similar protection running on either side of the body. It was suggested that part of the roof could be made from detachable fabric. The seating arrangement indicated that the idea for the car came about before the SIA competition was established, since the rules demanded two seats only.

The concept behind the SIA competition was to produce an affordable design, a people's car, and at the same time revive the depressed French automotive industry, which at the time was catering only for the diminishing and saturated luxury car market. It was hoped that a massive stimulation of demand would bring about a recovery. The competition rules asked for a car with a low selling price of f8,000 (only half the cost of a middle-

Le Corbusier and Pierre Jeanneret:
Voiture minimum model, plywood,
1989. (Design Museum, London)

range car). It had to have a closed, two-seater sedan body, an average speed of 75kph, and it had to be able to travel 100 kilometres on no more than five litres of petrol.

The Voiture minimum drawings (all undated except one marked 31/1/36) are lodged under the year 1936 in the Fondation Le Corbusier archives. They show that the car design developed over several years and progressed after the submission for the SIA competition. Though the proposed design was advanced in 1928, it was less so by 1935. The Voiture minimum proposal numbered 102, the last to be submitted, was described in the SIA album published in June 1936: 'The authors point out that as far back as 1928 they conceived a type of car, which they did not consider presenting at that time because it was too different from the accepted idea of the moment; showing the engine at the rear, aerodynamic forms, small bulk, yet great interior comfort. The main aim was to assure the maximum comfort for the passengers; the mechanical and structural characteristics must yield to this fundamental requirement.'[65]

Other well-known designers, such as Jean Edouard Andreau, Emile Claveau and J A Grégoire, also submitted concepts for the SIA competition, which was seen as a great showcase for French automobile design. In the end, no winner was chosen out of the 102 entrants, the main problem being their failure to achieve the prescribed selling price. Ultimately, it was the Italians who probably benefited most by developing the two-seater Fiat Topolino 500, designed by Dante Giacosa, Rodolfo Schaeffer and Mario Revelli de Beaumont in 1936.

Ronald Aver Duncan

Duncan (1889-1960) studied at the London Architectural Association before the First World War and was a lecturer there between 1917 and 1922. In 1922 he entered into partnership, establishing a practice called Tubbs, Duncan & Osburn in High Holborn, London.

Duncan was the author of *The Architecture of the New Era*, published in 1933, in which he presented his views on the future of architecture. He designed a number of houses and flats (including a house of the future for the 1933 Ideal Home Exhibition), as well as commercial and industrial buildings, exhibitions and interiors. He was also involved in the design of furniture and fittings. In addition, he designed car bodies for John Siddeley and Austin, and also proposed coachwork for several private individuals.

In 1922, Duncan was asked by John Siddeley (who had taken over Stoneleigh Motors Limited in 1912 while establishing his company, ultimately to be called Armstrong-Siddeley) to design a body for a light three-seater car with an air-cooled 1-litre, 9hp, V-twin engine with inclined overhead valves and aluminium pistons. It was to be called the Stoneleigh and the sale price was to be £100. Duncan proposed a simple, clean design with side panels made flush by omitting valances (the in-fill pieces between the running boards and the car body). The driver was placed centrally, with the two passengers sitting on either side, thus affording everyone the best possible view. The small Stoneleigh did not reach large production numbers, however, because of strong competition from cheap Morris cars and the Austin Seven.

Later, in 1928, Duncan designed a body called Merlyn for the Austin Seven range. The car, which was to sell

Ronald Aver Duncan: Stoneleigh, 1922.
Three-seater with a central driving
position.

for £185, had an all-weather-fabric saloon bodywork and a counterbalanced folding roof. Again, the valances and running boards were omitted, and the doors stretched the full depth of the body. The colour scheme consisted of a black bonnet, wings and top. The body was panelled in pale grey 'python-skin' fabric, with the seats in a cherry-red leather.

Joseph Emberton

A prolific British modernist architect of the 1930s, Joseph Emberton (1889-1956) was involved in producing an unusual body design for the innovative Lancia Lambda. Emberton studied architecture at the Royal College of Art in London. He worked for Trehearne & Norman and Thomas Smith Tait before setting up his own office in 1926, starting with interiors and product design and moving on to produce modernist architecture. He was the designer of the New Empire Hall in London (Olympia 2, 1929-30), the Royal Corinthian Yacht Club in Burnham-on-Crouch, Essex (1930-32), and the London Simpson Department Store (1935-36). In 1927, Emberton was commissioned by London's Lancia concessionaires, the Curtis Automobile Company, to propose a body for a three-seater, seventh series, 16hp Lambda. He was inspired by Vickers Vimy aircraft from which he borrowed a number of details. Lancia Lambda Airway was built on the short 3.1-metre wheelbase chassis in wood and aluminium, and covered in fabric by Albany Carriage Company of Hanwell. The aircraft connection could be seen in the slanted windshield, the wicker-framed, leather-upholstered seats, and the over-supply of dashboard instruments, including an altimeter and airspeed indicator. The elegant fastback profile reinforced by a unique rear three-window dormer, bestowed the car with an early attempt at streamlining, despite the typical vertical Lancia radiator. This design, which was the most famous Albany creation, with fire red and cream body fabric and red leather seats to match, was exhibited by Curtis on their stand at the 1927 Motor Show, where it was priced complete at £945. Although several chassis went to Albany for this bodywork, only one Airway is known to have survived, now in the USA.

Joseph Emberton: Lancia Lambda Airway with bodywork built by Albany Carriage Company, 1927. Standard equipment included a fan heater, radio, bar, Kodak camera and an air-speed indicator and spotlight on the roof.

Gio Ponti

Ponti (1891-1979), a prolific Italian architect and designer and editor of *Domus* magazine (1928-41 and 1948-79), was keenly interested in trains. He published a number of articles in his magazine discussing, for instance, Josef Hoffmann's train designs, American railways, or the Italian 1948 self-propelling observation car. With Giuseppe Pagano, Ponti worked on the 1933 Breda ETR 200 railcar prototype. Ponti designed the train's interior, producing high, adjustable seating with headrests almost like aeroplane seats in bright colours, arranged without compartmentalisation. The carpet had a pattern of intersecting geometrical panels, inspired by the de Stijl movement; radiators were covered in perforated metal sheets.

Between 1952 and 1954, Ponti designed, with the benefit of technical advice from Carrozzeria Touring di Milano coachbuilders, a car on the Alfa-Romeo chassis using his favourite diamond principle. (This principle was based on a highly intellectual concept, which led Ponti to work on a mix of cultural viewpoints as if looking

Gio Ponti and Giuseppe Pagano: Breda ETR 200 railcar prototype, 1933. View of the interior. (Archivio Fotografico Gio Ponti)

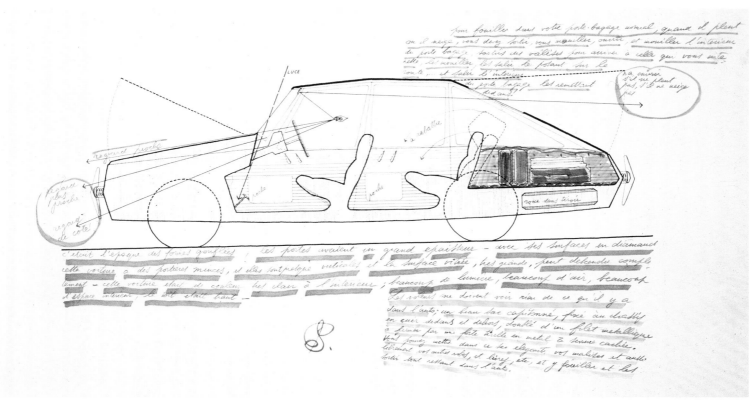

*Gio Ponti: advanced design of a saloon
car on Alfa Romeo chassis, 1952-54 for
Carrozzeria Touring di Milano. Sketch,
side and top views. (Archivio
Fotografico Gio Ponti)*

into a kaleidoscope through which the world could be seen in diamond or hexagonal shapes. The result was a multitude of elements produced from the fusion of patterns and materials.) His idea was to achieve maximum space and minimum encumbrance, increasing accessibility within the car and improving the driver's field of vision. His design was a reaction against the car styling of the day, which Ponti considered 'swollen, of inflated forms, full of empty spaces, with very high radiators, tiny windows and dark interiors'.[66] The skin panels were flat and stiffened with folds, not ribbing. The roof was low, and large windows surrounded the perimeter of the cabin. The doors were elegant and slim, almost vertical, with windows that could be rolled down. Rubberised, springy bumpers at the front and rear and white rubber strips on the side panels protected the body. The car had plenty of light and air thanks to the light-coloured interior, and, similar to Ponti and Pagano's ETR, it had adjustable seats and a boot that was accessible from the inside and separated from the spare-tyre compartment. A note on one of Ponti's sketches says: 'If you want to search in the regular boot when it is raining or snowing, you must step out of the car and get wet, then open the boot and get the interior of the boot wet, take out all the suitcases in order to find the right one, get them wet and dirty, because you need to stand them on the ground, and you dirty the inside of the boot when you put them back again!'[67] For Ponti, the car had to be beautiful: 'A car too is made to be looked at: like the gondola.'[68]

Feeling that Ponti's design was too far ahead of its time, Touring lacked the courage to propose it for production – yet Ponti's body form is similar to the range of Saab cars developed more than forty years later from Sixten Sason's design for Type 99 of 1960.

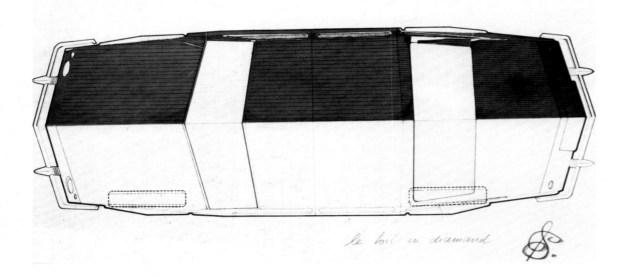

le toit en diamant

Richard Neutra: perspective views of a bus proposal for White Motors Company, 1931. Neutra was not allowed to progress too far from the established lines of the period. (Department of Special Collections, Charles E Young Research Library, UCLA)

Richard Neutra

Neutra (1892-70) was born in Vienna, where he studied at the Technische Hochschule, qualifying in 1917. There he met Adolf Loos and was influenced by the work of Otto Wagner. In 1923, Neutra moved to the US, where he initially worked for Frank Lloyd Wright and with Rudolph Schindler. His early American masterpiece was the Lovell House in Los Angeles (1927-29).

In 1931, Neutra met Philip Johnson's father, the lawyer and financier Homer H Johnson, who lived in Cleveland. Johnson was a company attorney and a major shareholder in the Aluminium Corporation of America. He was trying to persuade White Motors Company to use aluminium in the design of a new bus and was searching for a suitable designer. At that time his son, Philip, was busy designing and setting up a new modern architecture exhibition at New York's Museum of Modern Art, which included some of Neutra's projects. When Homer asked his son if he could recommend a designer, Philip suggested Neutra. Neutra was astonished by the proposal as he knew nothing about buses, but, because work during the Depression was scarce, he was eager and willing to learn.

Johnson senior accommodated Neutra in his private club in Cleveland and paid him a generous fee of $150 per day. The in-house designers at White Motors were somewhat conservative and Johnson was keen to bring in an outsider. However, they were resentful of Neutra's intrusion and put obstacles in his way throughout his stay in Cleveland. In a letter to his mother-in-law, Neutra complained about his difficulties: 'I have drawn up beautiful buses against the involved special interests of the various bureau chiefs ... The chassis specialist advises me to round out, to make the rear more exotic; that affects only the body designer and not him, but the radiator cannot be tampered with under any circumstances ... I have discussions with the bumper, the aluminium seat and upholstery experts ... '[69] Neutra also realised that if the bus was to find buyers, his proposals must not be radical or differ too much from the stylistic fashion of the day. In a letter to Rudolph Schindler, he stressed: 'Do not believe that great departures from the normal will be admissible.'[70]

In the United States, and even in Europe streamlining was not used seriously in the manufacture of passenger vehicles until 1933-34, and Neutra's design hardly suggested this dynamic expression of movement. Instead, the bus had a simple, unadorned form with an upswept back and a wave motif over the roof of the driver's cabin. The radiator remained square and vertical with headlights fixed to the front wheel wings, which were separated from the body. Neutra produced several alternatives. Manufacture did not materialise and not even a prototype was produced. The Depression and the inflexibility of the White Motors directors put a stop to further development.

Norman Bel Geddes

'We enter a new era. Are we ready for the changes that are coming? The houses we live in tomorrow will not much resemble the houses we live in today. Automobiles, railway trains, theatres, cities, industry itself, are undergoing rapid changes. Likewise, art in all its forms. The forms they presently take will undoubtedly have kinship with the forms we know in the present; but this relationship will be as distinct, and probably as remote, as that between the horseless buggy of yesterday and the present-day motorcar ... Today, speed is the cry of our era, and greater speed one of the goals of tomorrow.' So begins *Horizons*, the book written and published by Bel Geddes in 1932.

Norman Bel Geddes: car number 1, study series for Graham-Paige, 1928. The first stage of advancing design to be completed gradually into the final proposal in five one-year phases. (The Norman Bel Geddes Collection, The Theatre Arts Collection, Harry Ransom Humanities Research Center, The University of Texas at Austin, by permission of Edith Lutyens Bel Geddes, Executrix)

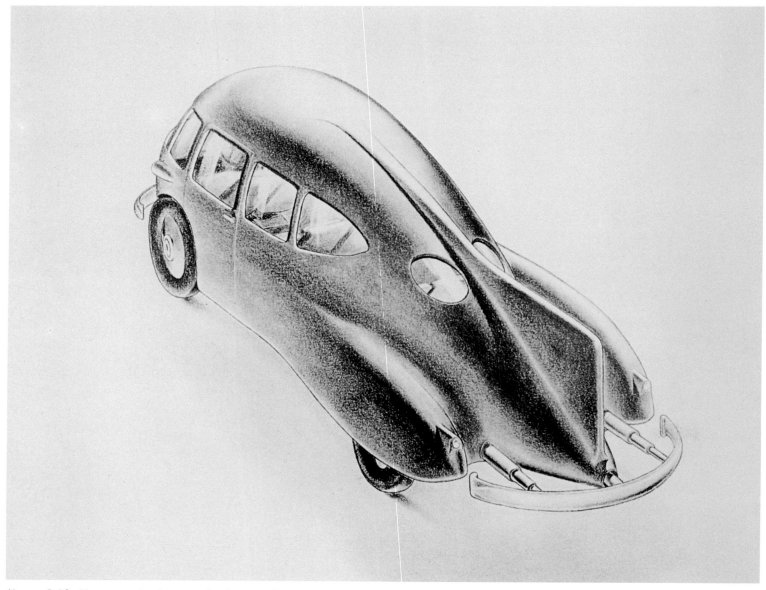

Norman Bel Geddes: car number 8, perspective view, 1931. (The Norman Bel Geddes Collection, The Theatre Arts Collection, Harry Ransom Humanities Research Center, The University of Texas at Austin, by permission of Edith Lutyens Bel Geddes, Executrix)

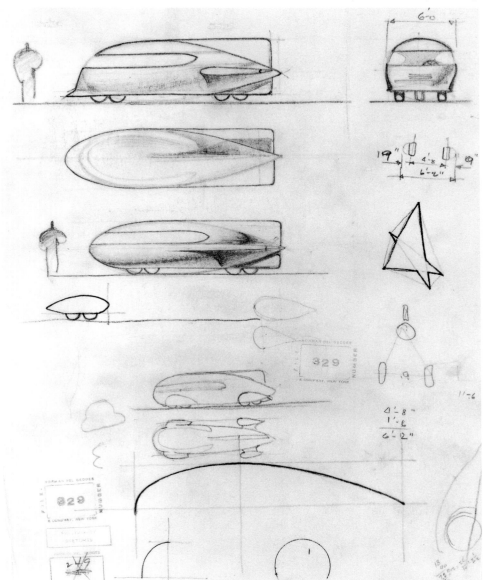

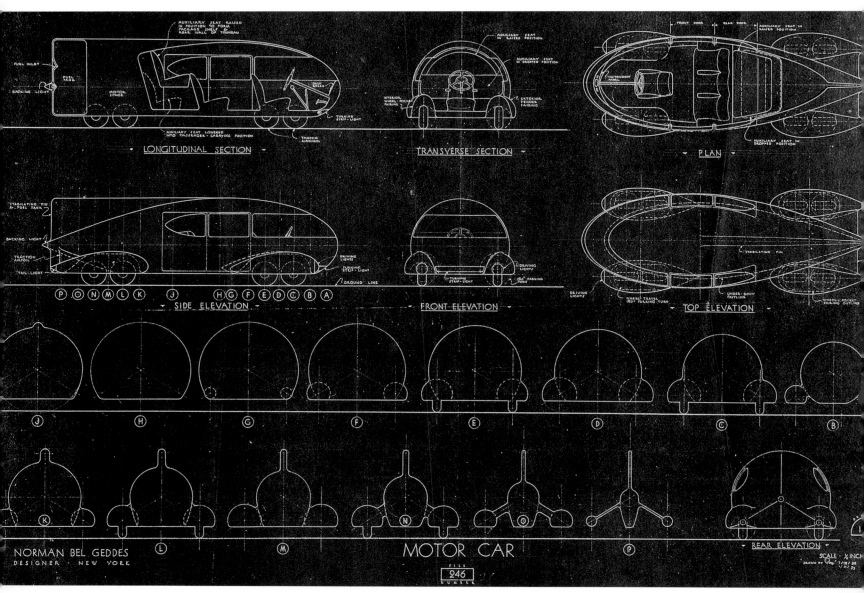

Norman Bel Geddes: car number 9, blueprint drawing, 1932. (The Norman Bel Geddes Collection, The Theatre Arts Collection, Harry Ransom Humanities Research Center, The University of Texas at Austin, by permission of Edith Lutyens Bel Geddes, Executrix)

Bel Geddes (1893-1958) was not a qualified architect. Initially, he worked as an illustrator and advertising agent but during his life, devoted much of his time to stage and theatre design and the construction of innovative exhibition halls such as the Futurama building at the 1939-40 New York World's Fair. He first became interested in architecture in 1916, when he worked with Frank Lloyd Wright on the design (never realised) of the Barnsdall Theatre in Los Angeles. He was even more profoundly affected by his 1924 meeting with Erich Mendelsohn, who gave him a sketch of the Einstein Tower and a copy of his new book *Structures and Sketches*. Bel Geddes found Mendelsohn's dynamic architectural designs inspiring, and was especially impressed by his 1919 lecture 'The Problem of a New Architecture', in which Mendelsohn suggested that all new architectural form had been based on inherited form and tradition. Then came the first iron girder, inspiring an exalted feeling of liberation – suddenly there was recognition of the dynamic tension of construction in steel and concrete. Inspiration arose, said Mendelsohn, not from past tradition, but from the example of the design of machines and engines of transportation. Later, Bel Geddes wrote that architecture, more than any other art form, expresses the spirit of the time in which it is created.

When his theatre and stage design commissions dwindled in the late 1920s, Bel Geddes set up an industrial design service. He realised that the commercial and industrial world was more interesting than anything that was happening in the theatre. From then on, Bel Geddes was involved not only with car design, but also with proposals for coaches, trains, aeroplanes, ships and vacuum cleaners as well as exhibition pavilions, car showrooms, hotels and theatres. From 1940, he worked for Nash Kelvinator, developing proposals for refrigerators, kitchen units and vehicles. Hardly any of his car concepts and modifications were ever realised, but his approach and notions influenced future generations of designers. One of his most revolutionary ideas was for a motorway network skirting major urban areas with several lanes dedicated to vehicles with differing speeds, and with electromagnetic command systems regulating the traffic flow. However, Bel Geddes considered that even the best-built roads would not be able to cope with increased future traffic and one of his last projects indicated a solution. In 1945 he designed a futuristic car with telescopic retractable wings, which enabled the vehicle to take off and fly to its destination like an aircraft.

For all his designs, Bel Geddes followed an established procedure. He would determine the precise performance requirements for a product, study the methods and equipment used in the client's factory, keep the design programme within the budget, consult experts on the use of materials, study the competition and conduct consumer-use surveys on existing products in the field. Only when all this had been done would he proceed with drawing studies. For Bel Geddes, the design process was essentially a matter of thinking; graphic presentation came only as its confirmation. 'Design is a process of thinking – not a thing unto itself. It is the essential step in any successful activity ... The most important part of an industrial design job is the thinking that is done before any drawing or even a preliminary sketch is made ... I am first of all interested in human beings.'[71]

In his 1931 book *Der Mensch und die Technik*, the German writer Oswald Spengler wrote that machines only serve a process and originate in the thought of this process – all means of transportation have been developed from the thought of travelling, rowing, sailing or flying, not from the image of a carriage or a boat. Bel Geddes took on board Spengler's lesson and began his designs with the thought of making speed comfortable. For him, speed and its effect on the means of transport were the starting point. 'In the development of transportation and speed we have reached that point where design is increasingly important from the viewpoint of efficiency and safety.'[72] For Bel Geddes, speed was the expression of modernity, creating transitory, fleeting impressions and affecting all solid objects by translating the vertical static line into a horizontal dynamic force.

Bel Geddes believed – mistakenly, along with many others – that a falling drop of water had a teardrop shape and as such was an inspiration for the streamlined form. Paul Jaray, in an article published in 1924,[73] pointed out that the falling drop of water is essentially spherical and would need fins and stabilisers to be stable. (Streamline designers later used the term 'suspended' or 'hanging' drop of water, but as such, it had nothing to do with movement.) Nevertheless, Bel Geddes succeeded in developing streamlined forms for his vehicles without the use of wind-tunnel testing. The variety of his impressive road vehicle designs can be seen by studying the photographs of the Futurama animated traffic exhibit intended for the New York World Fair of 1939-40.

One of his first commissions, in 1927, which came from Ray Graham of the Graham-Paige Motor Company, was to design an ideal automobile form for five years in the future. Both men were interested in streamlining ,but knew that the general public was not yet ready for such an avant-garde development. So Bel Geddes designed five cars, one model to be produced per year, each one increasing the degree of innovation in order gradually to familiarise the public with the new designs. Car number one was almost conventional, but it suggested the beginnings of smooth curves to the bodywork and revealed Bel Geddes' desire to join all the individual parts into a single continuous form.

Bel Geddes studied contemporary car designs such as Cord, Packard and Franklin, learning about front-wheel drive, diesel engines and air cooling. From this research emerged some more advanced proposals, such as car number eight, which had eight seats and a rear engine enabling the centre of gravity to be lowered, improving the relationship between the weight of the car and its load. In addition to stabilising the car, the back fin also acted as a petrol tank. In 1933, Chrysler asked Bel Geddes to carry out studies for the Plymouth Airflow, as well as improvements to the body of the new Chrysler Airflow and the De Soto.

Traditionally, body, chassis and engines were all separately designed by individual manufacturing sections, and the designer did not have a free hand in considering the car as a whole and complete unit. However, when Bel Geddes designed a car, he first considered the body form and only later defined the chassis structure, power unit and its position. This is the approach used by most car manufacturers today, with one factory department generally controlling all the design elements.

Norman Bel Geddes: the flying car, model, 1945, the last known Geddes' car design.
(The Norman Bel Geddes Collection, The Theatre Arts Collection, Harry Ransom
Humanities Research Center, The University of Texas at Austin, by permission of
Edith Lutyens Bel Geddes, Executrix)

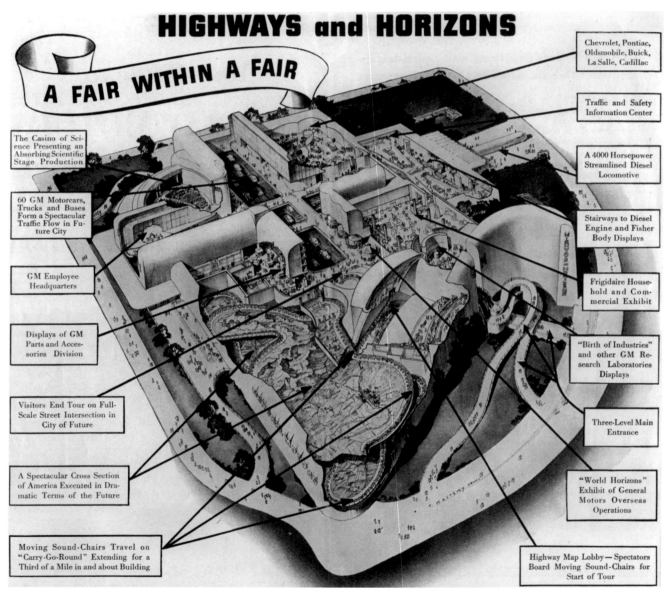

HIGHWAYS and HORIZONS

A FAIR WITHIN A FAIR

Chevrolet, Pontiac, Oldsmobile, Buick, La Salle, Cadillac

Traffic and Safety Information Center

A 4000 Horsepower Streamlined Diesel Locomotive

Stairways to Diesel Engine and Fisher Body Displays

Frigidaire Household and Commercial Exhibit

"Birth of Industries" and other GM Research Laboratories Displays

Three-Level Main Entrance

"World Horizons" Exhibit of General Motors Overseas Operations

Highway Map Lobby — Spectators Board Moving Sound-Chairs for Start of Tour

The Casino of Science Presenting an Absorbing Scientific Stage Production

60 GM Motorcars, Trucks and Buses Form a Spectacular Traffic Flow in Future City

GM Employee Headquarters

Displays of GM Parts and Accessories Division

Visitors End Tour on Full-Scale Street Intersection in City of Future

A Spectacular Cross Section of America Executed in Dramatic Terms of the Future

Moving Sound-Chairs Travel on "Carry-Go-Round" Extending for a Third of a Mile in and about Building

Norman Bel Geddes: General Motors pavilion, which included the
famous Futurama – a view of the USA in twenty years time – at the
New York World's Fair 1939-40. Schematic layout.

Richard Buckminster Fuller

'The captain of Spaceship Earth',[74] Buckminster Fuller (1895-1983) was a proponent of continuous technical development, which builds on past achievements, marching ruthlessly towards the future.

He was seven years old when he saw an automobile for the first time, actually driving one when he was twelve. When he was nine the Wright brothers invented the aeroplane but he did not see one until he was fourteen years old and only flew in one when he was twenty-three. As a boy he made paper dart models, then box-kite-like multi-plane gliders.

In later life, Buckminster Fuller owned successively fifty-six automobiles, three of which he invented and built himself. He drove a total of one and a quarter million miles, and flew one and a half million miles part of that distance in three of his own planes. Buckminster Fuller considered the automobile a broken-off part of the house. He believed that 'automobiles are little part-time dwellings on wheels. Both autos and dwellings are complex tools... component tools within the far vaster tool complex of world-embracing industrialisation.'[75]

In 1928, Buckminster Fuller decided to group his various inventions – houses, planes, cars and so on – under the title 'four-dimensional thinking' or '4-D', a term meant to express his overall concern for humanity, time and space. Later, in 1929, he used another word, 'Dymaxion', which was made up of the words he used most frequently when lecturing – 'dynamic', 'maximum' and 'ions'.

It was also the name of an important project that came about at around this time: the Dymaxion House. This was a revolutionary design. In its final version the Dymaxion House had hexagonal tension-suspended floors hung from a central structural mast. The top play-deck was shielded by a streamlined Duralumin roof, which protected people below from the weather; the masthead contained lenses for utilising the sun's rays; the area under the suspended house was intended as a 'hangar' and garage enclosed by venetian blinds; a worm-gear elevator was placed in the body of the mast; and the internal doors were pneumatic, opening and closing by interrupting the light beam of a photoelectric cell.

Buckminster Fuller later recalled that 'more and more people were beginning to get excited about my Dymaxion House. My idea had been air-deliverability of the house with all its autonomous equipment – the whole thing weighing only three tons – to be installed in very remote places without highways or runways for airplanes. You could set down the Dymaxion House like a bird landing on a rock someplace, and it could be anchored by cables to keep it from blowing over. So I turned my attention to transport, to developing a vehicle that would take you back and forth from these remote places.'[76]

An important idea on which Buckminster Fuller worked at around this time was the 4-D Triangular Auto-Airplane. This consisted of an aircraft fuselage with front wheels, rear-steering wheel and rudder. The concept of this vehicle, whose structure was based on Buckminster Fuller's favourite basic tools of the trade – the polygon, polyhedron and tetrahedron – was exactly what its name implied. It behaved like an automobile on the road, powered by two liquid air turbines attached to the front wheels, while the third turbine drove the front propeller, which enabled the fantastic car to take to the air. The pneumatic wings would be inflated by the forward

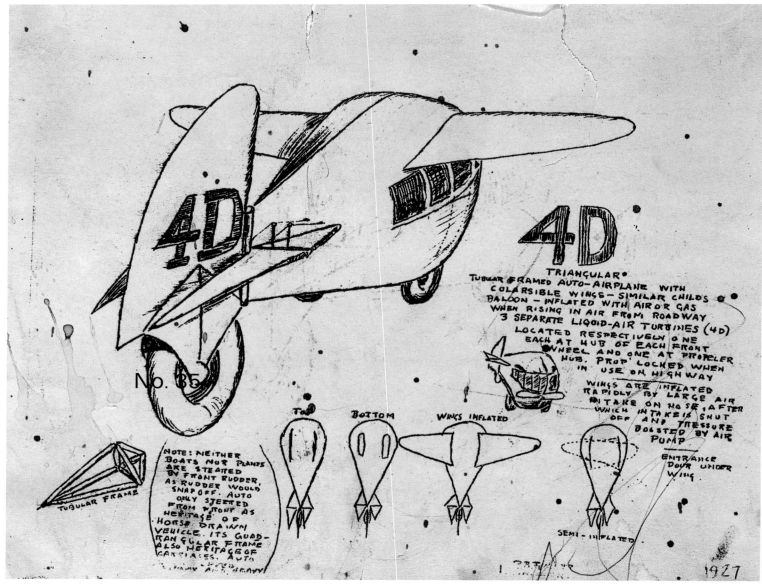

Buckminster Fuller: 4-D Triangular Auto-Airplane, 1928. A road vehicle with the ability to be converted with inflatable wings into a plane. (Buckminster Fuller Institute)

motion, helped by an air pump.

This idea became the basis for further development and in 1932 Buckminster Fuller came up with '4-D Transport', which had twin four-cylinder petrol engines and a triangular space-frame chassis enclosed in an aircraft-like body. The propeller and wings were omitted and a retractable rear steering fin was used at high speeds. This vehicle was intended to drive with its tail off the ground to achieve minimum contact with the road for comfort and smoothness. In the November 1932 issue of *Shelter* magazine, Buckminster Fuller explained that the car of the future had to be developed with minimum overall weight and it had to be streamlined.[77] From here, it was a natural step to the Dymaxion car in 1933.

Buckminster Fuller collaborated on the Dymaxion car project with Starling Burgess, whom he had met in August 1932. Burgess, an aircraft and yacht designer, had designed three Americas Cup defenders, including the victorious 1930 *Enterprise*, which featured a Duralumin mast and boom. Early in 1933, Buckminster Fuller and Burgess leased a disused Locomobile car factory in Bridgeport, Connecticut, erecting a large '4-D Dymaxion' sign above the main gate. A Philadelphia stockbroker, Philip Pearson, financed the project. He had a vision that the American automobile industry could help to pull the United States out of its depressed economic state if only a new revolutionary car could be created, as Henry Ford had done earlier with the Model T. A team of expert coachbuilders, metalworkers and woodworkers were employed on the Dymaxion project (and, to keep them fully occupied, also on Burgess' racing yachts), managing to produce the first Dymaxion car prototype in just four months.

The car, with the licence number FV 453, had a beautiful streamlined form with a curved, fixed, Perspex windscreen and windows, which followed the hand-beaten profile of the aluminium body panels fixed over an ash body-frame. The roof was covered with stretched yacht canvas. There was no rear window, the view behind being visible through a roof-mounted mirror. Only four seats were fitted – though the car could have accommodated up to eleven passengers – into a boat-like interior with the ash frame and ply panelling exposed. Everything, including the single front headlamp, was symmetrically arranged along the longitudinal central line.

The car was powered via a three-speed gearbox by a standard, 1932, Ford side-valve, 3.6-litre, 65bhp , V8, rear-mounted engine, which drove the front wheels.[78] The Ford engine normally achieved a top speed of 80mph and had a 16-miles-per-gallon fuel consumption. However, Buckminster Fuller figured that – although the Dymaxion was 5.7 metres long – with streamlining and a reduced kerb weight of 840 kilograms (1,850lbs), the speed could be improved to above 100mph and fuel consumption reduced to 22-30 miles per gallon. To achieve his aim, Buckminster Fuller hoped to bring down the frontal wind resistance to a quarter of that in normal contemporary designs. The main scissor-like frame, made from perforated steel sections, was split from the rear to either side of the engine and the cabin. At the back, it accommodated a 160-degree-turning steering wheel. The idea of rear steering (Buckminster Fuller considered front-wheel steering a relic from days of the horseless carriage) was inspired by yacht design, fish, birds, and aeroplane manoeuvrability. The involvement of Burgess and the workforce's dual task meant that the Dymaxion car inevitably had a close relationship to racing yacht construction and marine technology.

'I knew people would call it an automobile,
but it wasn't designed to be just an automobile.
It was designed, as I said, to become an omnimedium,
wing-less, flying device
with angularly orientable twin-jet stilts –
like the jets coming out from beneath the wings of a duck.'[79]

*Buckminster Fuller: Dymaxion car number one, 1933, the most
elegant of the three created. When compared with other
automobiles of the time, Dymaxion looked like something from
outer space. (Buckminster Fuller Institute)*

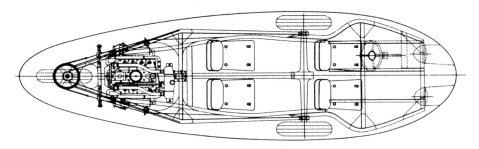

Buckminster Fuller: Dymaxion car number one, 1933, plan and section showing two headlights, which were used in Dymaxion car number two. (Buckminster Fuller Institute)

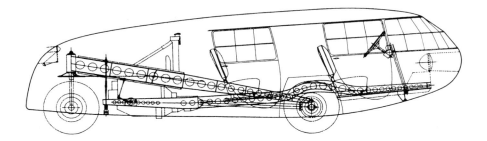

Buckminster Fuller: Dymaxion car number two, 1933, the only known surviving vehicle. (Buckminster Fuller Institute)

Buckminster Fuller: Dymaxion car number three, 1934, with the typical roof exhaust funnel, at the 1934 Chicago World's Fair with Buckminster Fuller at the wheel. (Buckminster Fuller Institute)

The second Dymaxion, completed in 1933, is the only known car by Fuller to survive and is housed in the National Auto Museum in Reno, Nevada. The car has a faceted windscreen, more windows with opening lights than the previous model, entry doors on both sides, two front headlights and a canvas roof changing to metal over the engine compartment. It was registered with the licence number SL 187. The third and last Dymaxion car, HF 349, completed in 1934, had a fin-shaped exhaust at the rear and an all-metal roof, and was the heaviest, weighing 1,360 kilograms (3,000lbs). This was the car exhibited outside Fred Keck's Crystal House at the 1934 Chicago World's Fair. Along with the house itself, and the Whiting Corporation's Nash Motors exhibit (the 'Nash Tower of Value', a tower of plate glass enclosing a paternoster lift in which Nash Sixes and Eights – six- and eight-cylinder cars – kept moving up and down, day and night) the Dymaxion caused a sensation.

Buckminster Fuller drove the English writer HG Wells around New York in the Dymaxion. Whenever they stopped, crowds immediately came running from both sides of the street and surrounded the car. Wells was surprised that he was not recognised. 'It is quite amazing to find myself here and nobody pays the slightest bit of attention to you or me. They act as if it's their car, as if the car belongs to them.'[80]

The Dymaxions were extraordinary motorcars, well ahead of anything else at that time. Their pure, streamlined form must have appeared like something from science fiction. Although they owed their concept to the work of other pioneers of streamlining - such as Paul Jaray and the Tropfenwagen, designed by Edmund Rumpler in

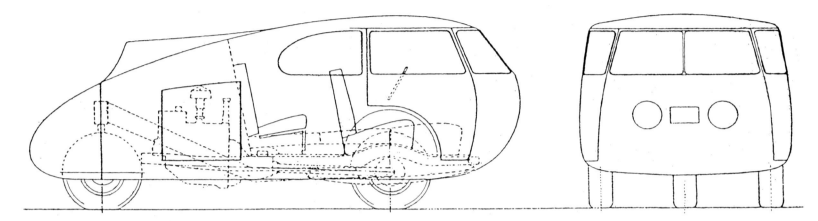

Buckminster Fuller: Tudor Sportster
design, late 1930s.
(Buckminster Fuller Institute)

1921, Emile Claveau's 1926 Voiture de Caractère Aérodynamique, Zeppelin airships and Junkers aircraft – Dymaxion cars advanced the idea of streamlining. At the time, America was behind Europe in terms of aerodynamic design, and very few besides Buckminster Fuller were experimenting in the field, among them Norman Bel Geddes, and the aircraft designer William B Stout with the Scarab car (1932), later followed by Raymond Loewy. The first streamlined American car was the unsuccessful Chrysler Airflow of 1934, designed by Carl Breer.

However, the technical and mechanical design of the Dymaxion car was flawed. Because of the three-wheel base and the rear single steering wheel, the car was unstable at speeds higher than 50mph, since the tail tended to lift off the ground and cause loss of steering. This problem was exacerbated by the weight distribution, because the front axle took three quarters of the car's mass. For the same reason, the braking power of the front wheels was not very effective. The Dymaxion was also sensitive to side winds. The long body transferred flexing into the frame, inducing camber changes to the rear wheel. The situation could have been improved if Buckminster Fuller had returned to the 4-D Transport design and fitted an aircraft tail and elevator unit. Though it was claimed that the Dymaxion reached speeds of 120mph, this seems unlikely given its instability and underpower. Even the highly scientifically streamlined Tatra 87 of 1936 designed by Hans Ledwinka and Erich

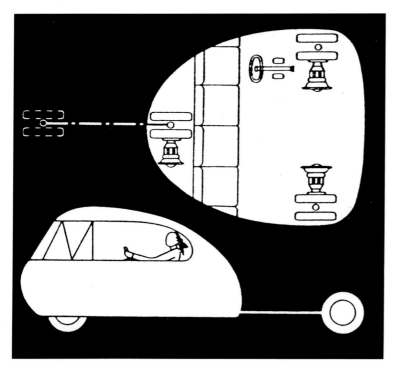

*Buckminster Fuller: D-45 car design
with three-wheel steering, 1943-1950,
plan side and perspective views.
(Buckminster Fuller Institute)*

Übelacker, which used Jaray patents and which was powered by a 2.9-litre, 75bhp, V8 engine and weighed 1,400 kilograms, could only manage a top speed of 100mph with a four-speed gearbox.

Confirmation of the Dymaxion's difficult handling characteristics came during car number one's test drive at the 1933 Chicago World's Fair 'A Century of Progress' exhibition. The driver of the Dymaxion, goaded into a race with another car, was rammed by it, and crashed outside the main gate, overturning. The canvas roof caved in, killing the driver and injuring the potential buyers (British aviation experts) who were in the car with him. Recorded details of the incident differ since reporters arrived at the scene after the car that caused it had left.

This unfortunate accident caused a loss of confidence in Dymaxion cars; Philip Pearson withdrew his backing and Buckminster Fuller himself had to finance the construction of cars numbers two and three, which were then in production. Despite these drawbacks, however, some American car manufacturers – Chrysler, Packard and Studebaker – expressed interest in carrying out further development in the hope that a new car design might help the American car industry. An investment group, Hayden Stone, together with the Curtiss Wright aircraft company, intended to finance a new Dymaxion to be built at the closed Pierce Arrow car factory. In the end, the deal was cancelled, but drawings of a 4.2-metre, four-seater Tudor Sportster and a smaller version of the same design as a single-seater car survived.

In 1943, the shipbuilder and car producer, Henry J Kaiser, asked Buckminster Fuller to design a car to be manufactured after the War. Together with engineer Walter Sanders, he proposed a compact three-wheeler car,

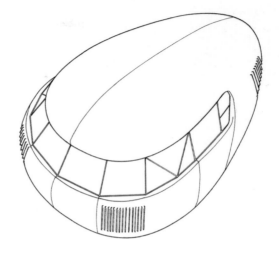

2m wide and 3m long, with a twin wheel at each point and an extendible rear boom for high speeds. With this car, called the D-45, Buckminster Fuller tried to overcome previous design difficulties. It had three small, air-cooled, radial, five-cylinder, 25hp, petrol engines, each one driving twin wheels and two steering systems. The number of engines used depended on driving conditions, thus limiting fuel consumption and noise. A standard steering wheel controlled the front wheels at higher speeds, while a separate crank handle operated the rear wheel when parking. The body was intended to be of all-metal monocoque construction with a hydro-pneumatic suspension system. The long and heavy wheelbase of previous designs was substituted with a reduced-size, lightweight, in-line four-seater compact cabin and an extendable boom achieving the same overall ground contact layout. In a later version, the D-45 exchanged its petrol engines for gas turbines. An overall weight of 440 kilograms was anticipated. A single engine prototype of the car without the extendible boom was tested in 1946 but production did not follow.

Buckminster Fuller's involvement in car design extended over almost two decades, leaving an important inheritance for future generations. He stressed the need for all design to produce objects useful to mankind, in step with the progress of technology, easily manufactured, and accessible to all. The dedication in *Streamlines*,[81] a book by his friend, Chris Morley, reads: 'For Buckminster Fuller, scientific idealist, whose innovations proceed not just from technical dexterity, but from an organic vision of life.' Norman Foster, a collaborator and great admirer, wrote in *The Architect's Journal* in 1995: 'What was never talked about was his poetic, sentimental and deeply spiritual dimension. That, in the end, was what for me his life was all about.'[82]

Giuseppe Pagano: Breda ETR 201 railcar, 1936, with clean, simple streamlined form. Exterior, front and interior view of the cabin and the kitchen galley.

Giuseppe Pagano

An Italian architect, theorist, furniture designer and editor of *Casabella* (1931-45) and *Domus* (1941-42) magazines, Pagano (1896-1945) believed that the goal of designers was to find the 'type-form': the absolute, anonymous, primary volumetric synthesis, the difficult but necessary achievement of an expression of simplicity. Pagano was an advocate of mass-production and the maximum use of modular systems in prefabricated building, exhibition design and furniture construction. His architectural designs expressed extreme rationalism and simplicity. 'If we want Italian architecture to continue in a direction that can be developed both aesthetically and morally, and if we want it to express our world, we must not think, act and poeticise with feelings that are aristocratic, eccentric or proudly enamoured with rationalised speculation. Rather, we must strive to be anonymous, to free ourselves from rhetorical attitudes. We must not imprison ourselves in an academy of forms and words.'[83]

Pagano worked for the Italian railway company Breda, designing carriages, rail cars and train interiors. For the Fifth Triennale di Milano in 1933, he presented, with Gio Ponti, a prototype for the new, fast, electric Breda rail car – the Elettrotreno Rapido 200. Pagano was responsible for the design of the exterior body, proposing a driver's cab with a simple, perfectly aerodynamic, triangular front, which blended smoothly into the rest of the long body. Ponti designed the interior.

In 1936, Pagano designed the Breda ETR 201, which was an update of the previous prototype, intended to run on the Bologna-Rome line. The rail-car had ninety-four seats, a rational arrangement of interior lighting and was air-conditioned. The cars were powered by six electric motors capable of producing a speed of 160kph. The train was displayed at the New York World's Fair in 1939.

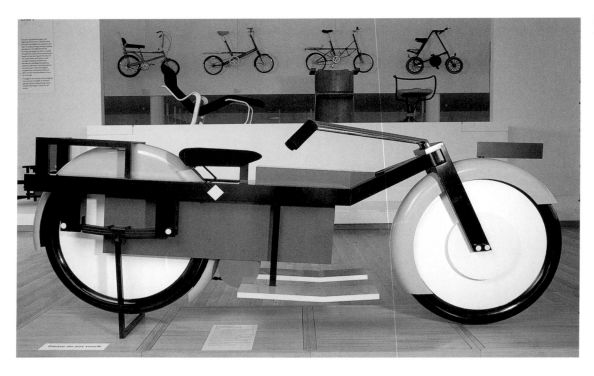

Werner Graeff

Graeff (1901-78) was born in Germany and studied at the Bauhaus in Weimar. Between 1922 and 1930, he was a member of the Dutch group of artists and architects known as de Stijl. As well as being involved in the design of car bodies and motorcycles, Graeff invented the international road-sign language. He maintained that new creativity must resolve all life's challenges with new means, not those derived from existing solutions. He also refused to separate art from technology, insisting that they had to work together. Putting his faith in technology, the future and progress, his aim was to create for universal requirements in contemporary life.

In the early 1920s, Graeff proposed several designs for motorcycles, automobiles and ship hulls. Some of these designs have disappeared and cannot be traced, though Graeff's skill can be appreciated thanks to surviving drawings of a motorcycle, conceived in true de Stijl fashion, and of a small, streamlined car whose form broke away from de Stijl principles.

The motorcycle design, from 1922, shows a significant departure from contemporary industrial styles. Graeff proposed a totally new construction according to his philosophy of always using new means: he replaced the traditional tubular-steel frame originally derived from the bicycle with a frame made from a pressed-steel sheet formed into a U-shaped section. It was a novel idea, influenced by this new material, achieving improved stability and flatter construction as well as better disposition of individual parts and concealment of fuel distribution. (Most of these principles were later taken up in motorcycle manufacture.) Individual parts of the body were painted with different colours, based on the established, pure de Stijl philosophy. From the initial, functional, technological object, Graeff had also created a pleasing work of art.

When Graeff tackled the design of a small automobile in 1923, he did not want to create a reduced-size version of a large automobile. Instead, he decided to start from the beginning, proposing the smallest possible weatherproof car for two persons. His aim was to create a sofa on wheels. Separating all the necessary elemental parts – the steering, seating, power unit and body – he assembled them in a new way. Well in advance of contemporary design, the Graeff body was effectively a streamlined, teardrop shape with a front seat for two and a dickey seat for an extra passenger above the centrally positioned engine. The aerodynamic design of the car body, which went against de Stijl's abstract, right-angle principles, caused some debate among the members of the group.

In 'On the Form of the Motorcar' (1925-26), Graeff wrote critically about Ford cars, which he felt were too conservative. 'For the past fifteen years we have known that there is an alternative, that a handsome car does not go any worse than an ugly one. And even more important, that the cost of manufacturing a pleasantly shaped motorcar need not in theory be any higher than that of a tasteless-looking one. We can demand a little intelligence and taste from the manufacturer in return for our money, and expect to pay no more for his hard work than for his negligence.'[84] Graeff stressed, moreover, that the shape of the motorcar should be preserved above all when it is in motion, because the smoothest line is ruined when the car jolts over an uneven road surface on solid rubber tyres: 'Our nerves demand pneumatic tyres and our aesthetic sense too.'[85]

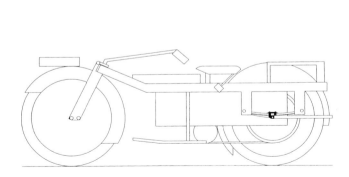

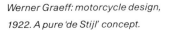

Werner Graeff: motorcycle design, 1922. A pure 'de Stijl' concept.

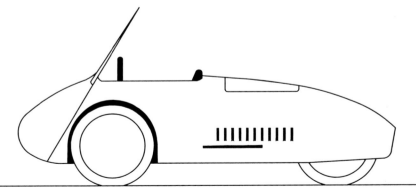

Werner Graeff: small automobile design, 1923, a highly advanced idea for that time.

Jean Prouvé

Prouvé (1901-84) was a versatile designer, combining the skills of engineer, constructor and architect. Most of his ideas were so far ahead of their time that they remained unrealised, and he spent much of his life misunderstood and unacknowledged, in the background, teaching future generations of designers and advising other architects. Prouvé summarised his position: 'It is not suitable to celebrate foolishly the engineer, who on occasions gives his knowledge into the services of an architect, but what if he himself is an architect?'[86]

Prouvé perceived that science and technology, applied to industrial production, would result in the possibility of rational change in living standards without affecting the priority given to problems of aesthetics. For him, beauty was born out of an object's conformity to the function it had to fulfil; style had no validity on its own outside the conceptual process; the correct solution was of value only from the point of view of objective conditions of production; and harmony between conception and execution proved the quality. Prouvé was convinced about two basic points: first, that in architecture the observer is affected by the detail, not by the overall view; and second, that the new soul of each era is always manifested by technical development.

Prouvé was greatly interested in cars and their construction, and for his lectures he borrowed car parts to illustrate how attitudes of the automobile industry could be transferred to architecture. Admiring the machine aesthetics embodied by the automobile, in 1930, he designed a cabriolet body. Later, in the 1950s, he considered designing and making his own car and worked on sketches for a prototype. When he bought cars, he chose luxury models – either a Voisin, a Salmson or a Triumph. Impressed by the Citroën Traction Avant monocoque body construction, he tried to apply the same ideas to the mass-production of housing, using corrugated and folded steel sheets.

With the capacity to mass-produce – to emboss, mould and cast – the automobile industry could produce dwellings that would have original architecture and be dynamic, believed Prouvé. It was, he felt, essential that

Jean Prouvé: lecture sketches of automobile bodywork executed during his teaching at Conservatoire National des Arts et Métiers between 1957 and 1970. (From Prouvé, Cours du CNAM 1957-70, Pierre Mardaga, Liège, 1990)

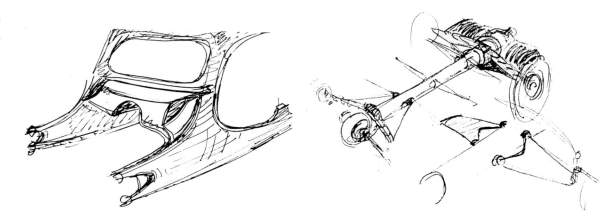

although these houses should not look like automobiles they would benefit from automobile technology, which was evidently economical. By likening the dwelling to a car, Prouvé saw the building as an industrial product including all the associated processes. Moreover, to deal with the problem of obsolescence, the house needed to be demountable and replaceable. 'Today the dwelling has to be dynamic. One of the greatest brakes of progress is a definitive house, which encumbers its site and prevents evolutionary urbanism. The dwelling has to be a consumer product, destructible, replaceable, and tradable in one or two generations.'[87]

Prouvé was most prolific between 1944 and 1954. In his Maxéville workshop he produced prefabricated houses, schools, furniture and building components. Important individual designs included the Niamey Tropical House, Meudon House, the 1951 Shell House and Alba House. In 1954, his workshop merged with the Société de l'Aluminium Français and his independence ended. From then on, Prouvé worked as a consultant to other architects and designers and taught at the Conservatoire National des Arts et des Métiers in Nancy. There, he observed that no substantial progress was being made either in architecture or in the building industry towards the industrialisation of construction methods, which he so ardently advocated.

In the words of François Chaslin: 'From the window of the train taking him from Paris to Nancy he stares at a disorderly world, built as best one can, with obsolete methods; while wagons ... well, wagons are made of perfectly joined, glistening stainless steel plate.'[88]

Marcel Breuer

Although Breuer (1902-81) never designed an automobile, his furniture was heavily inspired by the design of bicycles. The Hungarian-born architect and furniture designer moved to Dessau in 1925 to begin teaching at the Bauhaus, becoming master of the furniture workshop. He believed that 'the appearance of objects depends upon the different functions they have. Since they satisfy our demands individually and do not clash with each other, they produce collectively our style. They are unified as a whole through the fulfilment of their individual tasks. Thus the question of our style is not one of conviction, but of quality. A chair, for example, should not be horizontal-vertical, nor expressionist, nor constructivist, nor purely practical, nor compatible with the table. It should be a good chair, then it will be compatible with a good table.'[89]

About the time he arrived at the Bauhaus, Breuer bought his first bicycle. He adored the simple but sophisticated machine with its chromium-plated handlebars and tubular-steel frame. His admiration for the bicycle and the beauty of the curves of its handlebars made him realise that tubular steel was flexible as well as strong, elegant and modern, and could be used in the production of furniture. Initially, he approached Heinrich Kleyer, the Adler bicycle manufacturer, hoping to persuade him to make furniture out of chromium-plated steel tubes – but Kleyer was so astonished at the notion he thought Breuer was drunk. Breuer then went to see the Mannesmann steelworks company, which had patented a cold-drawn, non-welded tube and which was willing to supply the necessary material.

From 1925 until the early 1930s, Breuer designed over a dozen types of chairs, tables and stools in chromium-plated tubular steel. Most of these designs – such as the Wassily armchair, originally called the 'steel club armchair' or in Bauhaus literature the 'abstract chair' (1925-29), and chairs B5 (1926-27), B33 (1927-28) and the nest of tables B9 (1925-26) – are now well known and are still being manufactured and used throughout the world. Initially, the furniture was made by Standard-Möbel in Berlin, a company founded by Breuer with the architect Stefan Lengyel. In 1928, Standard-Möbel was taken over by Thonet which continued manufacture of the designs. Breuer's tubular furniture was tested and prototypes developed in close collaboration with the Hugo Junkers aircraft factory in Dessau, which had built all-metal aeroplanes since 1915.

In 1928, Breuer designed the attractive B54 three-wheel tea trolley in tubular steel, its upper table conveniently arranged as a detachable tray. In the same year, he proposed a tubular-steel *chaise longue* covered in stretched-steel-threaded fabric (also invented by Breuer) and fitted to four bicycle wheels. This was 'powered' by a fifth, centrally positioned wheel, which had a cog and chain to 'drive' one of the side wheels. The design, which reinforced Breuer's enthusiasm for the bicycle, remained forgotten in a private archive, only to be discovered in 1984, when it was realised by the Tecta Möbel company and exhibited at the 1985 Triennale di Milano.

As soon as tubular-steel furniture had been invented, car manufacturers realised that it was an ideal structural material for car-seat frames. Mart Stam, also known for his designs of tubular-steel furniture, is thought to have been inspired by car seats such as the emergency folding cantilever seat made by Chr. Auer Co of Bad Cannstadt in Germany between 1910 and 1920. On seeing a similar seat in 1926, he remarked, 'One should build a chair like that.'[90]

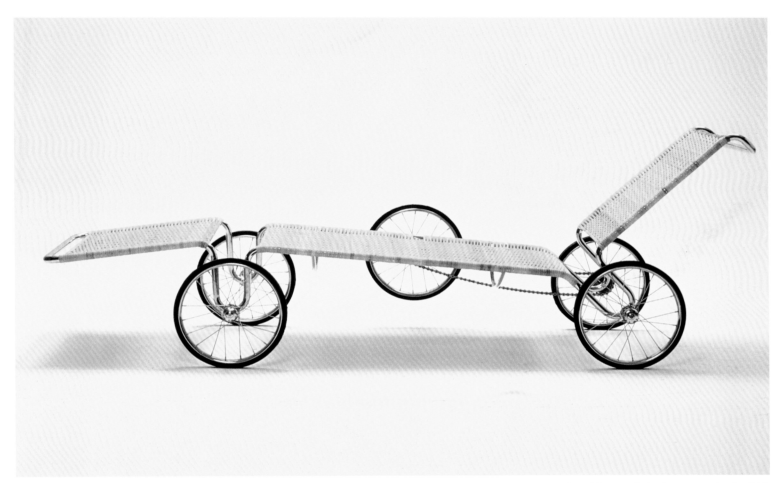

Marcel Breuer: chaise lounge on wheels, 1928,
inspired by bicycle architecture, re-created by Tecta
Möbel, 1984. (Tecta Möbel)

Carlo Mollino

Mollino (1905-73) was an individualist, an outstanding Italian architect and designer of furniture, interiors and, later, cars. He was acquainted with Le Corbusier and influenced by the work of Alvar Aalto. His machines looked like furnishings and his furnishings looked like machines.

Mollino was also a keen pilot and racing driver. His interest in aeronautics and car racing transferred readily to architecture: many of his structural elements, such as roof trusses and furniture frames, were derived from aeroplane wings and fuselages. Aircraft wing braces inspired the metal bracing of his furniture, while the use of tension struts in his designs was borrowed from the structure of aircraft hangars. His interest in existential minimalism stemmed from his experience of flying planes with small cockpits, which housed only the pure essentials. Mollino's architecture was, moreover, conjured up to create the sensation of flight. His best-known buildings are the Ippica Club riding school and stables in Turin (1937) and the Lago Nero Lodge, Sauze d'Ouix in Italy (1946).

In 1954, Mollino helped Mario Damonte remodel the Osca 1100 car, which participated in the Le Mans twenty-four-hour race in the same year. He also designed a model of a racing car with a large rear central fin intended for Ferrari. A year later, with Enrico Nardi and Damonte, he designed and constructed a stunning and unusual racing car, the Bisiluro ('Double Torpedo' or 'Twin-Boom') Damolnar. This project illustrated his obsession with achieving the ideal form, both in terms of function and expression of movement, and indicated his exquisite design sensibility. The idea behind the Bisiluro was to achieve maximum aerodynamic advantage by positioning the driver in line with one set of wheels, with the 735cc engine balancing the weight over the other side wheels, leaving the centre part of the car as low as possible. This clever arrangement used the booms – the parts of the car that needed to be raised to accommodate the wheels – to seat the driver and house the engine. The compulsory passenger seat (Le Mans rules demanded that each competing car should have two seats) was provided in the low, central part of the body. The chassis frame was made of tubular steelwork. In 1955, under the

Carolo Mollino, Enrico Nardi and Mario Damonte: Bisiluro racing car, 1955, schematic drawing and photograph. The 735cc, 60bhp, twin, overhead cam engine was built by Carlo Gianni.

Carlo Mollino and Mario Damonte:
Osca 1100, 1954.

Carlo Mollino, Enrico Nardi and Mario Damonte: Bisiluro Damolnar racing car (Nardi), 1955, built for the La Mans race. Mollino (in the driver's seat) designed the body, while the chassis was the responsibility of Damonte and Nardi. Its bold concept initially worried the other competitors. (Fondo 'Carlo Mollino', Archivi Biblioteca Centrale di Architettura, Sistema Bibliotecario, Politecnico di Torino)

company name Nardi, the Bisiluro – finished in the typical Italian racing red – took part in the 750cc category at Le Mans but was forced to retire during the race. The Bisiluro was called an 'absurd extreme ... one of the smallest cars, a twin-boom Nardi, was probably further removed from honest "prototype" intent than any entry before or since, but was accepted in spite of the "conform to the spirit" clause.'[91] Nowadays, the Bisiluro can be found exhibited in the Leonardo da Vinci Science Museum in Milan.

With Franco Campo and Carlo Graffi, Mollino then produced a design for the Nube d'argento ('Silver Cloud') exhibition coach for Agipgas (1954). It had an extendable display and canopy arrangement on cables to create a message when the coach was moving and a spectacle when stationary.

Mollino's interest in automobiles was reflected especially in his architecture of drive-in and drive-through buildings. His project for the Turin Chamber of Commerce (1964) incorporated a car-parking space at first-floor level directly connected to the road by a ramp. In his 1965 design for a theatre in Cagliari, the parking was on the roof, again accessed by a road and ramp. The drive-in Monte dei Paschi Bank (1972) in Turin let cars pass through the building via circular ramps to all floors, allowing customers to carry on their business without abandoning their cars. In 1956, Mollino designed an exhibition stand for Vis, a safety glass manufacturer, at the Salone dell'automobile in Turin using a red cold cathode tube outlining a car in one sweeping uninterrupted line. A contrasting yellow tube indicated an object hitting the windscreen of the car and being safely deflected by the glass.

Carlo Mollino, Enrico Nardi and Mario Damonte: Bisiluro (Double Torpedo or Twin-Boom) racing car, 1955. Mollino tests the spaceframe chassis, which tended to flex at high speed. At Le Mans the car was driven by Damonte and Roger Crovetto. (Fondo 'Carlo Mollino', Archivi Biblioteca Centrale di Architettura, Sistema Bibliotecario, Politecnico di Torino)

Carlo Mollino with Franco Campo and Carlo Graffi: Nube d'argento (Silver Cloud) exhibition coach for Agipgas, 1954. (Fondo 'Carlo Mollino', Archivi Biblioteca Centrale di Architettura, Sistema Bibliotecario, Politecnico di Torino)

Carlo Mollino, Enrico Nardi and Mario Damonte: Bisiluro Damolnar racing car, 1955. (Fondo 'Carlo Mollino', Archivi Biblioteca Centrale di Architettura, Sistema Bibliotecario, Politecnico di Torino)

Norman Foster

Foster (b. 1935) is a global architect, travelling the world, following in the footsteps of his hero Buckminster Fuller, erecting buildings on every continent as if there were no boundaries. Foster sees buildings as machines endowed with soul. His own constructions are precision-made and manufactured in parts off-site. Like the elements of expensive Swiss watches, which are supplied to the mother factory by various makers, they are eventually assembled into one perfectly functioning machine.

Foster's architecture is sharp and highly engineered, employing the latest technology transferred from a variety of innovative industries and giving the impression of being made by machines for their own use. The limited palette of neutral grey, white and silver applied to his architecture is symbolic of machines, engines and motors. His architecture comes alive with the people for whom the buildings are intended, and who add colour, movement and emotion.

In recent years, Foster has driven a black BMW 730i, a metallic brown Jaguar Sovereign and a black 1997 Range Rover 4.6 HSE. He spends his spare time building a large-scale model of a Ferrari, though on the whole, he prefers flying his Cessna Citation jet. His love of aircraft was revealed during one of the programmes in the *Building Sights* television series shown on BBC1 in March 1991. Instead of talking about a favourite building, as most of the personalities appearing in the series had done, he chose to talk about the Boeing 747. Foster's interest in aircraft developed in his youth when he made model aeroplanes. During his military service as a mechanic with the RAF, he worked in grass-covered aircraft hangars (a clear influence on his Willis Faber building in Ipswich and the Duxford American Aircraft Museum) on electronic systems for the Vulcan bomber. He was also a member of the London Gliding Club at Dunstable Downs.

'As a child I lived in a private dream world where my domain was the interior of a make-believe aircraft. Because my knowledge was limited to aeromodelling, I would repetitively sketch cross-sections in which I was perched on top of vast coils of elastic; by controlling a system of cranks and pulleys I would command the world's largest rubber-driven aircraft and fly off to the most improbable corners of the earth. I rediscovered a new generation of model aircraft when my elder sons were growing up. The edges of my later private world of solitary flying – racing sailplanes or flying in aerobatics competitions at a modest intermediate level – became blurred in the fantasy world of a sketchbook or my equivalent to counting sheep on a sleepless night.'[92]

Foster is always sketching and doodling – on memos from his partners, on the back of envelopes, or in his sketchbooks, which he carries with him everywhere – transforming a bicycle into a drinks trolley, sketching new forms for gliders or a rocket-driven, single-person racing car.

In 1992 he was asked to design a vehicle to provide access for disabled and less able visitors to the Royal Botanic Gardens at Kew, London. The project was funded by the Robert and Lisa Sainsbury Charitable Trust. The Sainsburys had admired the electric open platform train system in the gardens at Versailles and suggested that a similar idea should be developed in London.

Foster's priority was to design a type of transport that would not use a 'degrading' means of hoisting the

Norman Foster: Solar Electric Vehicle for the
Royal Botanic Gardens, Kew, 1992, exterior
view, drawings. (Richard Davies)

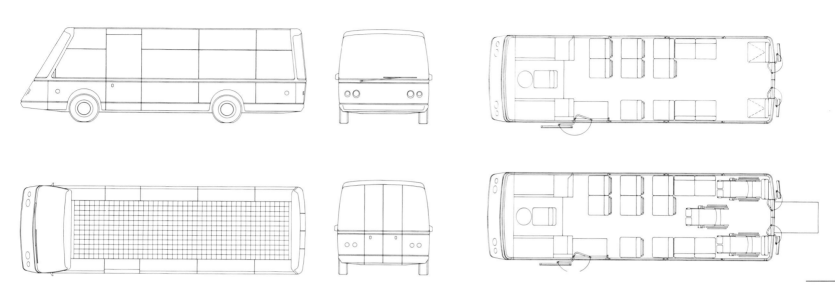

Norman Foster: Jetmobile sketch.
Aircraft analogy is never far from
Foster's mind.

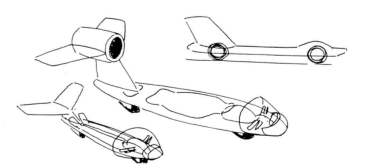

Norman Foster: M Y Izanami *yacht,*
1991-93, built by Lurssen shipyard,
Bremen. (Ian Lambot)

disabled people on to the moving vehicle. His idea was to design a mobile miniature conservatory, 'a big glass bubble', inspired by the Richard Turner and Decimus Burton Palm House at Kew. The maximum use of glass would allow an unhindered all-round view of the gardens. The power unit and fuel supply had to be ecologically friendly and conform to the surrounding green environment. The other inspiration came from the architecture of the Citroën SM, the curved VW Transporter, the faceted body of the 1943 German military SdKfz 251 armoured vehicle and the 1966 British Army Stalwart vehicle. The result — now in operation at Kew — is a twelve-seater minibus with two spaces for wheelchairs and a central driver position. For its power supply, one third of the energy is passed on from the photovoltaic cell-bank mounted flush to the roof with the rest coming from rechargeable batteries within the chassis of the bus.

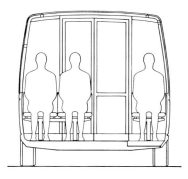

The cross section of the body is governed by the minimum radius of the glass side windows that curve onto the roof to increase the field of vision. The side windows can be fully opened to provide direct contact with the outside as well as extra ventilation. The body panelling is of a modular design made from a high-impact-resistant glass-fibre-reinforced, polyester and foam, composite sandwich construction. The front has a sharp faceted outline typical of Foster, giving the vehicle a 'razor-edge' front buffer. Loading and disembarking is by soft air suspension, which lowers the bus at the rear; the short extendible rear ramp then leads the wheelchairs into the interior. Independent rear wheels on trailing arms let the flat interior floor become part of the ramp. The air suspension also lowers the side entrance to a single step height, allowing easy entry on foot. The low centre of gravity provides a smooth ride, eliminating roll in the bends. The electric 10hp power unit achieves 12mph and a 12-kilometre run per day.

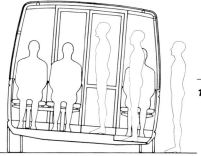

The cost of the vehicle came to £80,000. However, a number of elements had to be bargained for, such as the curved glass and the photovoltaic cells, with design and construction completed in ten months — a fraction of normal motor industry costs and time when developing a new model.

From the solar electric bus, Foster derived further ideas for a hybrid drive electric taxi (1993) as an alternative to the outdated diesel-powered London cabs. The taxi was designed with a small 250cc petrol engine operating at optimum efficiency and driving an electric generator, which supplied electricity to motors driving each wheel on the same principle as a lunar rover. The light metal space-frame chassis supported the glass-fibre reinforced composite body panelling.

Between 1991 and 1993, Foster also designed a 58-metre-long yacht, the *M Y Izanami*, with an aluminium hull. The sharp-faceted design is a semi-monocoque welded construction with an aluminium skin, frames and longitudinal stiffeners. Its elegant wheelhouse enclosure bears the triangular features that are characteristic of Foster's designs and which also appear in the backrest of the Kite Chair designed in 1997. The yacht was built in the Lurssen shipyard in Bremen, Germany.

Jan Kaplicky

Kaplicky (b. 1937) is perhaps the only architect who consciously tries to encompass automobile technology in his architectural creativity. Since the foundation of Future Systems, the architectural practice he set up with David Nixon in 1979, he has advocated the use of monocoque construction methods in the art of building. From his earliest projects – which unfortunately survive only on paper – his thoughts have been focused on the problem of how to transfer automotive, aircraft, naval and space technology to domestic as well as commercial and public architecture. For him, it is logical that the inspiration for innovative architecture should be sought in the most forward-reaching industries, those which employ the most advanced technologies. The industries concerned with automotive products constantly demand improvements in safety and comfort but at the same time pursue higher goals.

Kaplicky's buildings, though derived from sources of engineering technology, are first and foremost humanistic and organic in their origins. His machines are living organisms inspired by naturalistic forms and then turned into complex kinetic and robotic sculptures. Faithful to his Czech cultural heritage, Kaplicky is especially taken with the idea of robots conceived by two Czech writers, the brothers Josef and Karel Čapek. Like the Čapeks' robots, Kaplicky's robotic architecture is not mechanical and distant but closely attached and responsive to human emotions, aspirations and needs, fully complementing them like a tightly fitting glove.

Kaplicky has owned cars since his youth. In 1950, his father bought a Volkswagen jeep in which Jan learned to drive. Later, the family had a Ford Anglia, which was an unusual car to own in Czechoslovakia under the Communist regime, when cars – especially the Western-made models – were a scarce and expensive commodity. During his studies in the late 1950s, Kaplicky and some student friends bought a 1923 Laurin & Klement open tourer, made by the renowned Bohemian motorcycle and automobile manufacturer before it was taken over by Skoda in 1925. After he came to Britain in 1968, he shared a yellow Volkswagen Beetle with Eva Jiricná.

When he and David Nixon founded Future Systems in 1979, they envisaged that architecture would inevitably move towards the adoption of spacecraft technology. However, outside observers and architectural critics saw this as a step too far, too soon, and their projects remained unfulfilled dreams. In the mid-1980s, Kaplicky also found inspiration in pure organic forms and his architecture acquired a more naturalistic sense.

In 1983, he had proposed a redesign of the London Routemaster double-decker bus. His idea was to use a streamlined body shape on a long wheelbase chassis with four-wheel steering to achieve maximum manoeuvrability and seating space. Wide centre doors gave access to standing room only on the lower deck and seating only on the upper platform. The driver's cab was combined with the front-wheel drive engine, which was detachable for maintenance and servicing.

Then, in 1988, came his 'Drop' project – a short-stay accommodation unit for two people using two semi-monocoque GRP shells delivered by truck á la Bertrand Goldberg to a suitable site. The form of the Drop was clearly inspired by automobile body shapes.

Jan Kaplicky: the Drop project, 1988, inspired by automobile technology.

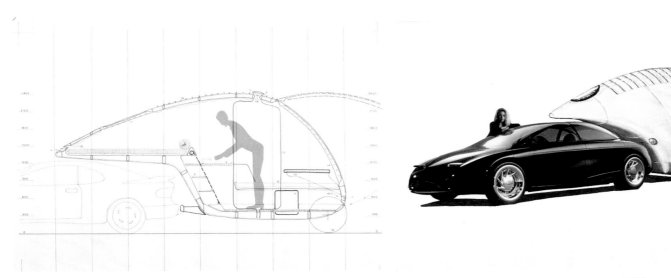

Jan Kaplicky: caravan, 1989, semi-monocoque construction. Designs and a view of the completed object.

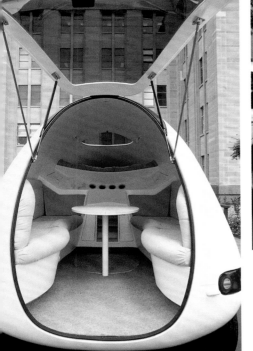

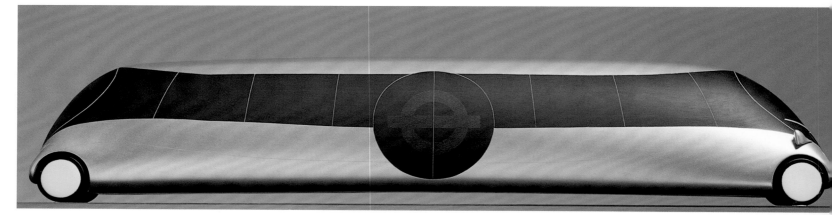

*Jan Kaplicky: Superbus, 1993-97, a
proposal for replacement of the current
range of single- and double-decker
London buses.*

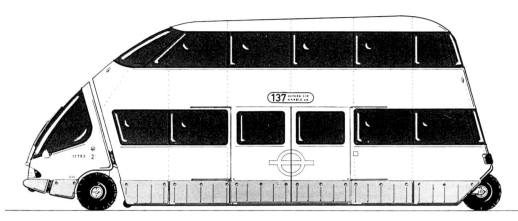

Jan Kaplicky: London Routemaster double-decker bus, 1983.

Jan Kaplicky: Superbus, 1993-97 in London.

Though neither of these designs was ever realised, another car-connected project was. In 1989, Craig Bremner, the curator of the Museum of Contemporary Art in Sydney, asked Future Systems, along with four other architectural practices, to devise a caravan as an exercise to explore new ideas in the design of everyday objects. Three years later, Future Systems' caravan was made by a glass-fibre boat-building company in Perth to fit snugly over a 1990 model of the Toyota Celica. By cantilevering the caravan over the car body, its overall length was reduced, allowing much improved manoeuvrability. The streamlined body was constructed of a semi-monocoque, 25-millimetre-thick compound sandwich structure with roof-mounted solar panels to provide electricity for its life-support system. A conceptually similar innovative trailer with a gooseneck extension, designed and manufactured by the American aviation pioneer Glenn Curtiss in 1919 and called Aerocar, was Kaplicky's inspiration, along with early prototypes of Airstream trailer.

Between 1995 and 1997, Kaplicky designed a small, 3-metre-long, three-seater city car with electric motors driving each wheel, and a bank of batteries located behind the rear seats. The driver's seat was centrally positioned with two passengers sitting behind on either side. The interior was accessed via a front-hinged door incorporating the panoramic windscreen. The body was made from semi-monocoque GRP or aluminium panels.

During the four years between 1993 and 1997, Kaplicky updated his previous bus design with a 13-metre-long, single-decker, ninety-passenger Superbus. In this proposal, the seating is arranged along the snaking perimeter, with entry doors positioned in the centre of the body. The wheels are placed at each extreme corner of the vehicle. Again, four-wheel steering gives the bus maximum flexibility and manoeuvrability. The bus has electric batteries, designed to be recharged at the final stops via a pantograph collector at roof level. Again, the driver is placed centrally. The body is made of aluminium panels. In comparison with the current articulated single-decker London bus, which is 17 metres long, the shorter Superbus, accommodating the same number of passengers, appears a much more attractive and suitable vehicle for the future of public transport in a large city.

Jan Kaplicky: small city car
project, 1995-97.

Renzo Piano

The Italian architect, Renzo Piano (b. 1937), is convinced that creativity derives from a deep knowledge and understanding of the materials and processes used to make an object. He believes that 'the designer has to invent the process, not just the finished product, and he has to design the tools too.'[93] For him, there is no separation between conception, materials and production. To produce good designs, all elements – including feedback from the construction process – must interconnect. Piano admires wood and models of objects made in this material, particularly the wooden models of car bodies from the 1950s. For Piano, these studies not only advanced the form but also helped in the development of the modern art of car-body building.

In 1978, Fiat asked Piano and Peter Rice, a structural engineer, to analyse the way in which it designed and manufactured its cars, and to indicate the kind of car that would be needed more than a decade later in the 1990s. Fiat's brief was the perfect challenge for Piano: to explore ideas for a light car that, if involved in a crash, would absorb energy without damaging the passenger compartment. According to Piano's design philosophy, this meant a total rethink of the way in which cars were made and a transformation of the automobile's image. To do this, Fiat founded IDEA, the research Institute of Development in Automotive Engineering in Turin, with Francesco Mantegazza as managing director, Piano as president and Rice as vice-president. A budget was fixed at 3.25 million dollars for a three-year programme.

Piano began by studying car assembly on the factory floor for six months. 'In the automobile works, all the various phases of the execution process come together. It is a great school for any architect.'[94] Piano and Rice then endeavoured to fulfil the basic functional requirements for a separation of the mechanical equipment from the area protecting the passengers. This led to a logical organisation of the vehicle using individual and interchangeable components – 'subsystems' as Piano called them – attached to an overall structural framework, establishing the skin and the skeleton.

The main goals were a reduction in weight and improved durability, safety and comfort. The whole concept of the car prototype, which was called the Vettura Sperimentale Sottosistemi (experimental subsystem vehicle), developed around these four issues, with weight being the most decisive one. Because of the heavy weight of the steel normally used in car production, alternative materials needed to be considered for the body panelling. They had to be tough but light, corrosion-free, repairable in case of accident and with a lifespan of at least twenty years. The best materials to meet these requirements were polycarbonate for the smaller panels (replaceable if damaged) and a repairable structural moulding compound, SMC, for the larger items.

For the frame structure, the ideal material was galvanised, spot-welded, gauge-type steel, which has torsional and flexile strength and can absorb crash energy. Tests on both physical and computer models investigated elastic and plastic deformation of the frame. At low speed, the crash energy was absorbed by two frontal elements that collapsed progressively; the main frame was designed to deform to take up the excess at higher speed. The frame was optimised using a mathematical pattern. The result was an overall saving of 20 per cent of the weight compared with a car made completely in steel.

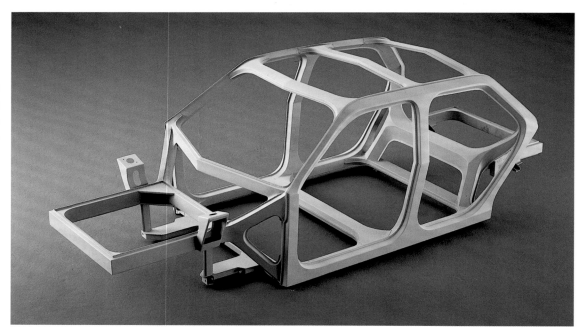

Renzo Piano and Peter Rice: Fiat VSS experimental car, 1978-80, the basic structural frame. (Renzo Piano Building Workshop, Genova)

Renzo Piano and Peter Rice: Fiat VSS experimental car, 1978-80, view of the final prototype. (Renzo Piano Building Workshop, Genova)

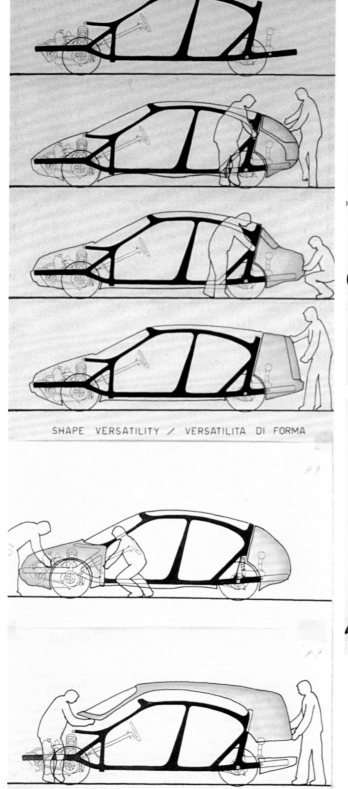

SHAPE VERSATILITY / VERSATILITA DI FORMA

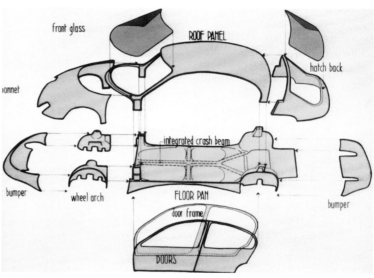

Renzo Piano and Peter Rice: Fiat VSS experimental car, 1978-80. The single frame offered a variety of bodywork applications. (Renzo Piano Building Workshop, Genova)

front glass   ROOF PANEL

bonnet   hatch back

integrated crash beam

bumper   wheel arch   FLOOR PAN   bumper

door frame

DOORS

109

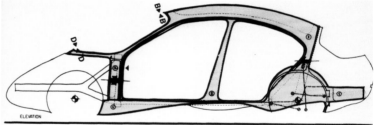

Renzo Piano and Peter Rice: Fiat VSS experimental car, 1978-80, schematic drawings of plastic body components. (Renzo Piano Building Workshop, Genova)

One benefit of using different cladding materials for the frame was a reduction in noise inside the car, since the plastic panels and the inclusion of acoustic barriers in the joints achieved better damping. Soft adhesive or nylon mechanical connectors were used in joining the panels. Another advantage of separating the frame and the skin was that a range of models and styles could be developed using the same common frame – so although the most expensive part of the body was unaltered, the cheap plastic subsystems could be modified to provide a great variety of coachwork enclosures. The same frame supported hatchback, saloon or estate bodywork. One fully functioning prototype of the Fiat VSS was manufactured and tested in the early part of 1980. When Fiat introduced its new model Tipo in 1988, many lessons learned from the VSS were incorporated. However, to modify the assembly line fully to the design principles proposed by Piano and Rice would have been too costly, as it would have required changing the complete production process. Piano admitted, moreover, that the design of the VSS was a compromise: it looked like a standard car 'so people would not be frightened. It is not the way it should have been done. If you follow the process, you end up with a car that is drastically different.'[95] What Piano had established was a car of a different nature from conventional designs. His car was no longer a finished complete and perfect object but a flexible technical element, which could be adapted to the specific requirements of the user.

Renzo Piano and Peter Rice: Fiat VSS experimental car, 1978-80, structural frame (below) and buckled frame member after test (above). Building construction could improve the quality of building components by adopting the automobile industry's approach to testing. (Renzo Piano Building Workshop, Genova)

As the VSS was being studied, Fiat asked Piano and Rice to find a use for 50,000 surplus engines, which they intended to donate to Morocco. As there was no motor industry in North Africa, Piano and Rice had to come up with a cheap, locally produced material that would enable the manufacture of a simple transport vehicle and provide a use for the engines. 'The Flying Carpet', as the project became known, was a truck with a standard platform for transporting people and goods, with the chassis bed made of ferro-cement combined with special resins. The assembly of the platforms with the less sophisticated parts was to be undertaken locally. The truck had a load capacity of 600 kilograms, including the driver; a range of body options could be fixed to the platform.

Both the VSS and the Flying Carpet proved to be beneficial for Piano, giving him an opportunity to exchange ideas at all levels with the motor industry and to transfer architectural techniques to them. At the same time, he was learning from automobile manufacture, gaining inspiration that he later used in architectural projects such as his winning competition design for a wind tunnel for Ferrari in Maranello, Modena, the construction of which began in 1996.

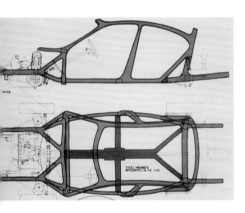

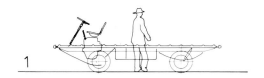

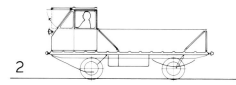

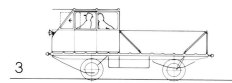

Renzo Piano and Peter Rice: Flying Carpet experimental truck, 1978, chassis elevation and possible body versions. (Renzo Piano Building Workshop, Genova)

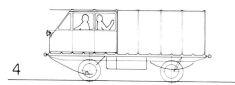

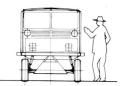

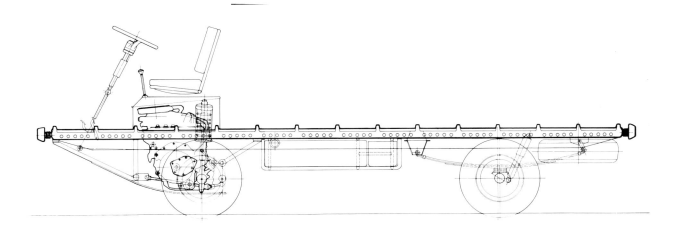

More Architects and Automobiles

Many other architects have been involved with automobile and automotive design. Jan Kotera, for example, an acknowledged founder of modern Czech architecture, was a student of and collaborator with Otto Wagner and the architect of a number of significant buildings as well as a designer of furniture, glass and china objects. He was influenced by HP Berlage, Frank Lloyd Wright and Josef Hoffmann. In 1898, Kotera was asked by Ringhoffer, a large Prague-based, railway-carriage and tramway manufacturer founded in 1771, to design a tramway car including the interior and seating. Another Czech architect Otakar Novotny designed an advertising car for the

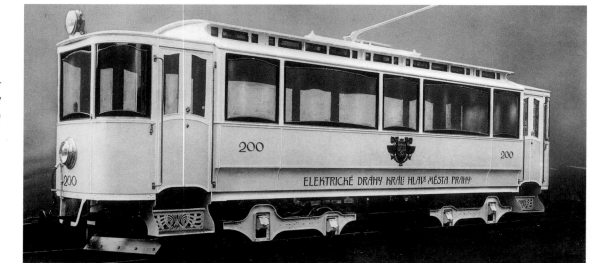

Jan Kotera: Ringhoffer tram for Prague, 1898. (National Technical Museum, Prague)

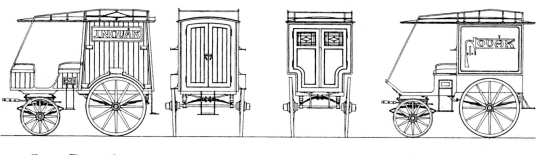

Otakar Novotny: study for a car carrying advertisements, 1910. (National Technical Museum, Prague)

André Noël Noël-Telmont: the 1931, 5.8 litre. 6-cylinder, model C22, 33CV Siroco 2-door coupé is considered his most beautiful Voisin. (from P Courteault, Automobiles Voisin, 1919-1958, White Mouse Editions, London, 1991)

J Novák company in 1910, still derived directly from the horseless carriage form.

The French entrepreneur, Gabriel Voisin, studied architecture alongside his friend, André Noël Noël-Telmont at the École des Beaux-Arts de Lyon in the late 1890s. Though Noël-Telmont became a fully qualified architect in 1899, Voisin failed to complete the course (in later life he liked to call himself an architect and mechanic). His first job was with a Parisian architect, but he subsequently started out on an independent career. He was nearly forty before he began designing cars, having already been involved in aviation, designing and producing at least ten thousand aeroplanes. He erected the first inflatable hangar buildings, was putting up prefabricated houses (which took just three days to build and furnish) as early as 1919, and designed a portable 200-seat theatre building. Noël-Telmont, who had meanwhile moved to Paris and learned to fly, helped Voisin in his construction ventures. After the First World War, when Voisin first established himself in automobile manufacture, Noël-Telmont was appointed head of the coachwork and body shop, and with Voisin became responsible for the design of all Voisin car bodies up to and including the C27 model. Voisin once wrote that a car without rational luggage accommodation was as stupid as a building without a staircase. Noël-Telmont left Avions Voisin in 1938 to devote his time wholly to architecture.

The Dutch architect Gerrit Thomas Rietveld, designer of the Schröder House in Utrecht (1924), proposed and constructed wooden toys in 1923: a hobble cart and a wheelbarrow made using a typical de Stijl approach, with bright primary colours.

Gerrit Thomas Rietveld: hobble cart,
wood, 1923. (Centraal Museum,
Utrecht)

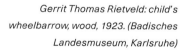

Gerrit Thomas Rietveld: child's
wheelbarrow, wood, 1923. (Badisches
Landesmuseum, Karlsruhe)

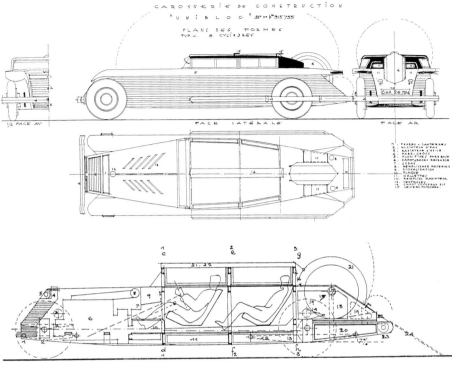

CAROSSERIE DE CONSTRUCTION
"UNIBLOC" Bté n° 315755
PLANS DES FORMES
TYPE 8 CYLINDRES

1/2 FACE AV.   FACE LATÉRALE   FACE AR.

COUPE A.B.

1 RADIATEUR D'HUILE	9 APPAREILS DE CONTRÔLE	17 SUPPORT ET BLOCAGE DE ROUES SEC
2 RESSORTS AV.	10 BOITE DE VITESSE	18 ROUES DE SECOURS
3 AMORTISSEURS	11 ACCUMULATEURS	19 VALISES SACS
4 RADIATEUR	12 TRINGLERIE ET RECHANGES	20 RESERVOIR
5 PHARE	13 RESSORTS DE SUSPENSION AR.	21 CAPOT ROUES SECOURS
6 BLOC MOTEUR	14 AMORTISSEURS	22 PLAQUE D'IDENTITÉ
7 CLOISON ISOLANTE ; PARE FEU	15 VALISES SACS	23 FEU ARRIERE
8 CONDUIT D'ECHAPPEMENT.	16 JAUDAS	24 PLAN INCLINE

Georges-Henri Pingusson: Unibloc coupé design, 1930, elevations, plan, section, perspective and bodywork schematic drawing. (Institut Français d'Architecture, Centre d'Archives d'Architecture du XXe Siècle)

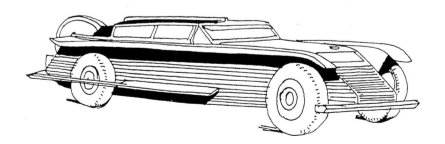

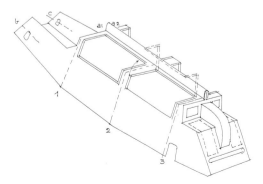

The French architect, Georges-Henri Pingusson, the designer of the National Monument to the Deported (1962) in Paris, proposed an unusual and advanced 4-5 seater, 8-cylinder 'Unibloc' coupé in 1930. The body skin was based on an idea similar to that developed by Jean Prouvé, using folded Duralamin sheets stiffened by structural 'bulkhead' members.

The Hungarians Gino and Oscar Jankovits from Fiume qualified as architects before studying engineering. They submitted a design for a streamlined sports car to Vittorio Jano, the legendary chief engineer of Alfa Romeo. The drawings were completed in December 1935 and showed a car with a central driving position – a popular proposal among architect car designers – with a long, sloping tail, which surrounded the mid-position engine. By 1937, the drawings had been developed into a prototype using an Alfa Romeo 6C 2300 engine. After testing and possibly some racing, the engine was changed to a 6C 2500 in 1938. This well-proportioned sports car is now in a private collection in Britain.

Gino and Oscar Jankovits: Alfa Romeo 6C Special, 1935, front and rear views, and a drawing showing the low body profile and mid-engine position.
(Michael Ware / Classic Cars)

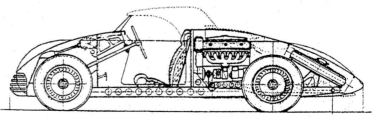

In 1936, the twenty-three-year-old American architect Bertrand Goldberg, who believed that 'function creates form', designed and produced a clay mock-up of the body of a rear-engine car. The design reveals the European influence of Paul Jaray's streamlined Ley, Audi, Maybach and Tatra. The mock-up was meant for a car with independent suspension on all four wheels. The chassis was to be fitted with a Ford V8 engine and pre-selective clutchless electric transmission. The automobile was intended to reach a speed of 140 miles per hour.

Bertrand Goldberg: clay model of a rear-engine car, 1936. Note that the model is moulded over a real chassis. (from M Ragon, Goldberg, On the City, *Paris Art Centre, Paris, 1985)*

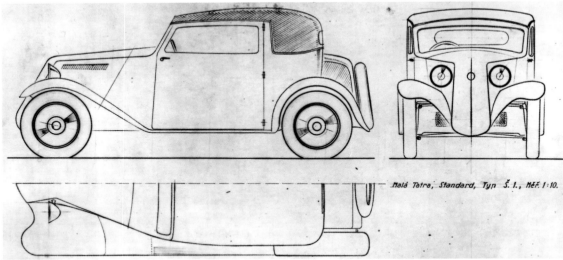

Lubomír Slapeta: Tatra 57, 1931.
(Vladimír Slapeta)

Malá Tatra, Standard, Typ Š. 1., Měř. 1:10.

The innovative Tatra Works in the former Czechoslovakia employed a number of architects to design its products. The architect Lubomír Slapeta, for example, sketched out a body design for the Tatra 57 in 1931; Frantisek Kardous was responsible for one of the prototypes of the spacious body of the rear-engine Tatra 603 (1956-63); and Vladimír Grégr designed the streamlined body for the Slovenská strela Tatra railcar (Slovak Arrow type M290) and railway passenger carriages B and C (1936).

Vladimír Grégr: Slovenská strela railcar, 1936, built at the same time as Pagano's ETR 201, exterior view and a contemporary poster advertising the fast travel time achievable between Bratislava and Prague. (Tatra Museum, Koprivnice)

Mario Bellini: Kar-a-Sutra minibus, 1972, with soft interior furnishing. The twelve-person 'mobile human space intended for human and not automotive rites'. Designed for an exhibition at The Museum of Modern Art, New York. (Mario Bellini Associati)

*Frei Otto: car design in combination
with tent structure, 1960-64.*

In Italy, Mario Bellini believed that while architecture had only minimal influence on the environment, the automobile had greater impact because it offered mobility, which improved life in many communities. He advised Lancia on car interiors for its models Beta and Trevi (1977-78), and designed the interesting Kar-a-Sutra minibus (1972), with a soft-cushion interior. Meanwhile, Ettore Sottsass was asked by Elio Fiorucci to redesign the Alfa Romeo Giulietta. However, Alfa Romeo rejected his natural look of Astroturf on the floor and painted clouds on the underside of the roof. In 1954, the designer Bruno Munari created colour schemes for Alfa Romeo cars, which were meant to dissolve in the air when glimpsed in movement.

Between 1960 and 1964, Frei Otto, a German engineer and designer of tensile structures, proposed a multipurpose motorcar. It was a family car with a spacious interior, reclining seats and a sliding roof that could be lowered. The windscreen was positioned well forward on the laminar streamlined body form. The car, which was equipped with an adjustable camping box, kitchenette and refrigerator compartment, was designed in combination with a tent structure for camping and to create a mobile home environment.

*Mario Bellini: Lancia Trevi, design of
the interior, 1977-78. (Mario Bellini
Associati)*

Guy Rottier, an architect of Dutch parentage living in France, worked for Le Corbusier as technical director for the Marseilles Unité d'habitation. In 1964, with Charles Barberis, he designed a holiday home in the form of a plastic-bodied helicopter. Called the 'Flying Holiday Home', it was meant as a manifesto for free expression in architecture, with free choice of materials and sites. This helicopter home gave its owner freedom and offered an escape from fixed locations and its associated laws and restrictions.

Guy Rottier: 'Flying Holiday Home' in the form of a plastic-bodied helicopter, 1964. (Collection FRAC Centre, Orleans, P Magnon)

Robert Opron: Citroën SM, 1970. The SM set a new standard in the streamlining of large, four-seater touring cars. Opron was also responsible for the Citroën GS (1971) and CX (1974). (Citroën)

The Frenchman, Robert Opron, was an architect by training, but he preferred to design cars. In 1962, he joined Citroën after completing three years with Simca and, in 1964, he succeeded Flaminio Bertoni as Citroën's chief of design. Under his direction, the car body for the model SM (1970-75) was developed, as well as successive Citroën GS and CX models. In 1975, Opron was enticed to join Renault, where he was made responsible for all Renault vehicles including coaches, trucks and tractors.

In the 1960s, many designers were preoccupied with urban megastructures and the consequences caused by the population explosion. They also turned their attention to the reduction of traffic congestion, often proposing different types of small car as the solution. The main problem with these designs was usually that they were based on the scaling down of a conventional car. One exception was the Quasar Car, conceived as a glass room on wheels. Unveiled in London in 1968, it was designed by the French inflatable furniture designer Quasar Khahn. Khahn understood that even a small car must accommodate its driver and passengers in comfort. The Quasar Car's rectangular tube chassis was built around two Austin Mini sub-frames, cut in two and widened by 125 millimetres. The chassis supported a flat, glass-fibre moulded platform, which carried a 50-millimetre square framework forming the main body structure. The glass body had double sliding doors on the sides and the front, and a single fixed panel combined with a glass-fibre panel below at the back using 5-millimetre safety glass. The roof had two panels of Triplex Sundym glass. The four-seater body was fitted with two separate front seats and a bench at the rear using Khahn's own inflatable transparent PVC cushions.

Quasar Khahn: Quasar city car, 1968. Mobile glass room with inflatable seating.

The Argentinean architect Emilio Ambasz designed an exhibition for the Museum of Modern Art in New York in 1976 called 'The Taxi Project', in which proposals for taxi vehicles tried to improve the design of urban transportation. In 1982, Ambasz, who believes that we create objects to satisfy the demands of our passions and imaginations, also reorganised an N14-litre diesel engine for the Cummins Engine Company into a sculpture.

After Alexander Calder's painted BMW 3.0 CSL was entered by Hervé Poulain in the Le Mans twenty-four-hour race in 1975, BMW decided to commission other well-known artists such as Frank Stella, Roy Lichtenstein and Robert Rauschenberg to colour the curved shape of the automobile body. The Spanish architect, sculptor and painter César Manrique was perhaps the most successful, choosing a flowing scheme of colours that enhanced the fast forward movement of the BMW 730i. The brightness of his scheme seemed to suggest the car's mobility while the skilfully shaped planes of colour emphasised the streamlined form of its body.

The flamboyant French designer and architect Philippe Starck proposed the Aprilia Lama scooter prototype

César Manrique: BMW Art Car Collection, model 730i, 1990. Perhaps the most successful artwork to truly enhance the car body of the BMW. (BMW (GB) Limited)

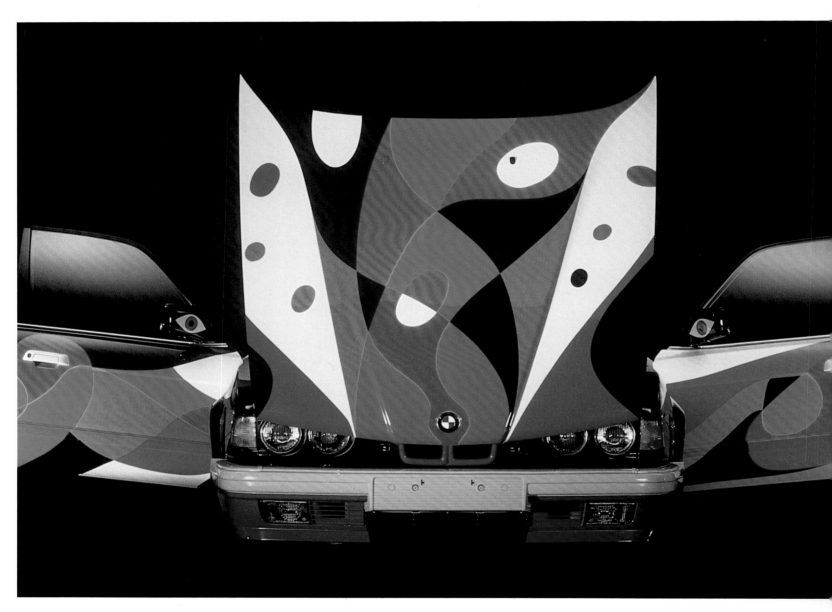

Philippe Starck: Aprilia X Ray 1000
motorcycle prototype, 1996. (Philippe
Starck, Paris)

Philippe Starck: Aprilia Moto 6/5
motorcycle, 1995. (Aprilia)

Philippe Starck: Lama scooter
prototype for Aprilia, Italy, 1992.
(Philippe Starck, Paris)

Philippe Starck: Toto and Plywood
car projects, 1996.
(Philippe Starck, Paris)

126

Naum Gabo: proposal for Jowett Javelin, 1943. Project carried out through the Design Research Unit. (From The Architect's Journal, *London)*

Luigi Colani: BMW M2 prototype, 1981. (from P Dunas,
Luigi Colani, *Prestel Verlag, Munich 1993)*

in 1992 and three years later designed a new motorcycle, the Aprilia Moto 6/5, which went into production. He also designed a prototype for the Aprilia X Ray 1000 motorcycle in 1996. In the same year he turned his attention to automobiles, proposing a three-door hatchback Plywood car and the Toto la Toto open fun car.

There are others who have designed cars and who have been mistaken for architects. Eric Broadley, for example, the designer of the Lola and Ford GT40 racing cars, was assumed by many to be a builder and architect but is in fact a non-graduate of quantity surveying.

Then there were the sculptors. The Italian Flaminio Bertoni, for instance, was the creator of the Citroën Traction Avant, the 2CV and the DS19. Through the Design Research Unit, founded by Herbert Read and Marcus Brumwell, on instruction from Jowett's chief engineer, Gerald Palmer, the Russian constructivist sculptor Naum Gabo proposed in 1943 a saloon body for a new model called the Jowett Javelin. Unfortunately, Gabo's 'jelly-mould' design proved too complex three-dimensionally for Jowett to manufacture. Based in Idle, Yorkshire, Jowett was a small company, which had to produce car body panels with minimum curvature to keep costs down.

Luigi Colani studied painting and sculpture in Berlin in 1946 and the science of aerodynamics at the Sorbonne in Paris. After his return to Germany in 1954 he worked on automobile designs for Alfa Romeo, Lancia, VW and BMW. Colani sees himself as an engineer and sculptor, and believes that nature has already solved all design problems. Fish, animals and organic objects are his inspiration, while his greatest artistic influences are the works of Henry Moore, Constantin Brancusi and Jean Arp. 'Straight lines have no right to exist' is his motto. His numerous designs for cars, racing cars, motorcycles, railcars, aircraft and trucks demonstrate his obsession with round and ovoid, positive and negative elements. Colani's most successful car designs include the 1959 GT

Luigi Colani: Utah 12 truck, prototype
with low drag coefficient of Cx
0.38,1989 and Utah 9 2CV speed record
racer, 1981. (from P Dunas, Luigi Colani,
Prestel Verlag, Munich 1993)

Erich Mendelsohn: factory for optical instruments, Fantasy project, 1917. (From B Zevi, Erich Mendelsohn, The Architectural Press, London 1985)

Erich Mendelsohn: car chassis factory, Fantasy project, 1915. (From B Zevi, Erich Mendelsohn, The Architectural Press, London, 1985)

Spider and the 1962 Lancia 1300 Spider. The forms of the truck cab prototypes Colani 2001 (1977) and Utah 12 (1989) fundamentally challenged the established contemporary truck body design principles. In 1977, he designed 'The Megalodon', a futuristic aircraft inspired by a shark's body.

Of course, there are also many architects who, though they have never proposed cars, have been greatly influenced by them or passionate about them. The German architect Erich Mendelsohn, for example, never designed automobiles or any other machines but his horizontal, dynamic building forms resemble automotive objects at a standstill. One of his sketches from around 1915 was for a car chassis factory. He found inspiration in photographs of the work of other architects, such as Henry van de Velde and Frank Lloyd Wright as well as from Werkbund yearbooks starting in the second decade of the twentieth century. Some of the feeling in his sketches was captured in his Einstein Tower built in Potsdam between 1919 and 1921. In 1923 Mendelsohn explained the horizontal emphasis, which translated into movement in his architecture: 'The vertical building creates the vacuum of use at its peak, and in its foundations the intolerable pressure of drudgery. Connecting such contradictory elements in series naturally creates revolutionary tensions and gradually yields to the horizontal tendency of parallel connection of elements in future production organisms ... Human beings of our day can find compensation for the excitement of their rapid life only in the tension-free horizontal. It is only their desire for reality that makes them masters of their unrest, and their haste can be overcome only by the most perfect rapidity.'[96]

Wells Coates, one of the leading figures of English modern architecture, received his PhD from London University for a study of diesel engines. A pioneer RAF pilot and a car-enthusiast, he owned a Leyland-Trojan and a Wolseley. During World War II he bought his favourite automobile, a 1926 Lancia Lambda, a four-seater open tourer. He believed that this car was 'more comfortable in its seating than most of the chairs you crowd into your tiny living room. When a prospective assistant turned up after the War and asked for a job, Coates told him to draw his car. The result was an impeccable measured drawing of the Lancia Lambda and a job for its draughtsman.'[97] In 1957, Coates proposed a mass rapid transit design, which included a four-seater miniaturised vehicle running on an elevated track inspired by the Mercedes-Benz 300 SL. The vehicle was entered from both sides, the whole top and side swinging upwards to open like the gull-wing doors of the Mercedes.

Just as some architects have designed cars, so some of the great car designers have dabbled in architecture, reinforcing the notion that there are strong connections between architecture and car design. In 1910, for

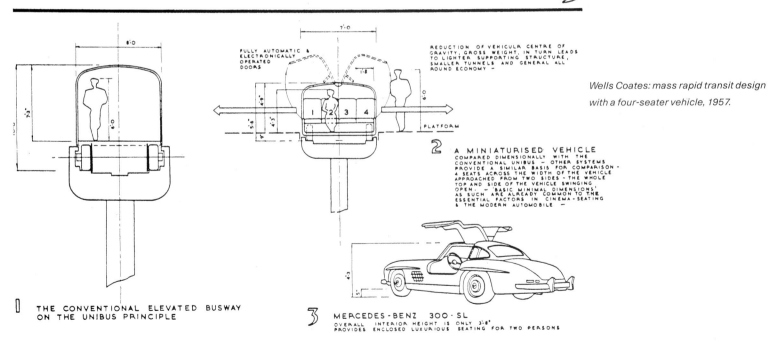

MINIATURISATION
THE OVERALL REDUCTION OF VEHICLE DIMENSIONS IN LINE
WITH ACCEPTED AUTOMOBILE PRACTICE
23

FULLY AUTOMATIC & ELECTRONICALLY OPERATED DOORS

REDUCTION OF VEHICULAR CENTRE OF GRAVITY, GROSS WEIGHT, IN TURN LEADS TO LIGHTER SUPPORTING STRUCTURE, SMALLER TUNNELS AND GENERAL ALL ROUND ECONOMY –

PLATFORM

2 A MINIATURISED VEHICLE
COMPARED DIMENSIONALLY WITH THE CONVENTIONAL UNIBUS – OTHER SYSTEMS PROVIDE A SIMILAR BASIS FOR COMPARISON – 4 SEATS ACROSS THE WIDTH OF THE VEHICLE APPROACHED FROM TWO SIDES – THE WHOLE TOP AND SIDE OF THE VEHICLE SWINGING OPEN – 'BASIC MINIMAL DIMENSIONS' AS SUCH ARE ALREADY COMMON TO THE ESSENTIAL FACTORS IN CINEMA - SEATING & THE MODERN AUTOMOBILE –

Wells Coates: mass rapid transit design with a four-seater vehicle, 1957.

1 THE CONVENTIONAL ELEVATED BUSWAY ON THE UNIBUS PRINCIPLE

3 MERCEDES - BENZ 300 - SL
OVERALL INTERIOR HEIGHT IS ONLY 3'-8" PROVIDES ENCLOSED LUXURIOUS SEATING FOR TWO PERSONS

example, Henry Royce of Rolls-Royce (by training, an electrical engineer) designed for himself La Villa Mimosa in Le Canadel near Le Lavandou on the French Riviera. Ferruccio Lamborghini proposed his own house with a gymnasium and indoor swimming pool in Casalecchio, on top of one of the hills overlooking Bologna.

The closeness of architecture and automobile design was confirmed further by the statements from contemporary car stylists revealed at the 'Moving Objects' exhibition held at the Royal College of Art, London in 1999. They found inspiration in the buildings and interiors of Frank Lloyd Wright, Frank Gehry (Guggenheim Museum, Bilbao, 1991-97) and William van Alen (Chrysler Building, New York, 1928-30).

Ideas and Reality

Having discussed the many innovative and visionary ideas and designs produced by architects for the car throughout the twentieth century, it is interesting to discover which vehicles they actually own, and why.

Indeed, the relationship between architects and their own cars was revealed in 1987 by the UK weekly architectural magazine, *Building Design*, when it published the results of a survey entitled 'What's Yours Called?'[98] Well-known British architects were asked what car they were driving at the time and why, and what would be their ideal choice. Sir Hugh Casson's first car, bought for £90 in 1947, was a 20hp Rolls-Royce (in choosing a Rolls-Royce he was following the example of Bannister Fletcher and Lutyens). Though he admired the Rolls-Royce, for its beauty, he claimed to have no love of cars and was not interested in what lay under the bonnet. At the time of the survey he was driving a Mini, which 'corresponds exactly to the Englishman's personal psychological bubble of the five-feet diameter in which he feels most at ease.'

Alan Phillips, meanwhile, liked to 'kick the shit' out of Ford Sierras for nine months without opening the bonnet, and his ideal choice was a different car for each day of the week to suit his varying moods. Fenella Dixon liked her VW Beetle for its character; in her opinion, it was the only car on the road composed of interesting smooth curves and which had individuality: 'The paradox is that the Beetle was produced as the ultimate mass-market car and it now survives as the car of eccentrics who happily wave and hoot at one another at the sight of a fellow sane human being.'

In Czechoslovakia in the late 1960s, Eva Jiricná's first car had been the plastic, unreliable, East German Trabant, not just the cheapest car on the market there, but the only one available in large numbers. In 1973, while living in London, she bought the new, bright yellow, 'unpretentious' Beetle that she still drives today. For her ideal car, she says, she will have to wait for someone to invent a small, maintenance-free car that is put together by a designer and a mechanic, just like the Beetle.

Interestingly, the *Building Design* survey revealed that, Robert Adam – despite his conservative architectural attitude – drove one of the most modern cars available, the Audi CD Avant. He admired its technology because it worked unobtrusively and well, and because most of its gadgets were automatic. Given Adam's architectural preference for classical elements clothing contemporary materials and technology, one might have expected him to prefer a Morgan or a kit car with a modern engine concealed by an outdated body design. Frank Lloyd

Wright would certainly have demanded that an architect's car be in keeping with his buildings. But would clients who demand to have their buildings designed in historical architectural styles, and the architects who oblige them, be satisfied with obsolete, out-of-date motorcars? One rather doubts it.

Other architects in *Building Design*'s survey were more predictable in their choice of car. John Townsend had a Citroën CX GTI, David Davies a Jaguar XJS, Jack Pringle a Ferrari Mondial V8, Michael Manser a Bentley TI, Max Hutchinson a Land Rover, David Rock an Audi Avant 100, Rick Mather a Honda Civic, John Lyall a BMW 316 and Owen Luder a Bristol Beaufighter.

Norman Foster was driving his third Porsche 911 Targa at the time. He likened this sports car to a modern antique, praising its good lines, reliability and responsiveness. However, he felt that it still left a lot to be desired: 'There are huge gaps in the car field. I'd like to see something really light, with proper use of storage, and power plant to maximise internal space, perhaps a new body fibre.' Foster preferred to drive a car with a ceramic engine, which would not rust, need lubricants or cooling, totally metal-free, light, beautiful, roomy, economical, quiet, pure in form and a delight to sit in.

Bryan Avery's car, meanwhile, was the reliable, economical, stylistically inert Vauxhall Cavalier Sri. Avery was the only architect surveyed by *Building Design* to propose his ideal vehicle, which he called The Avery Associates Architects Cellular Sedan. It consisted of three components: a front section with drive unit, a four-seat body unit and a rear end. The long-life safety-body cell-frame was the constant to all variations. It could be combined with a front interchangeable electric-, diesel- or petrol-powered motor with a range of outputs allowing DIY upgrading. Rear-end options could be selected from a hatchback, a saloon or an extra six-person dickey seat. So far no car producer has offered to manufacture Avery's design.

A more recent investigation in the *Financial Times* weekend magazine analysed the passion for cars of some other well-known architects.[99] This revealed that although James Stirling loved machines and cars, he was truly

4 door body cell with standard front end and boot back

4 door body cell with extended front and rear end

Bryan Avery: Avery Associates
Architects Cellular Sedan, 1987.

4 DOOR BODY CELL WITH EXTENDED FRONT AND REAR END

2 DOOR BODY CELL WITH SHORT FRONT AND REAR END

4 DOOR BODY CELL WITH STANDARD FRONT AND HATCHBACK

4 DOOR BODY CELL WITH STANDARD FRONT AND BOOT

4 DOOR BODY CELL WITH STANDARD FRONT AND 'DICKY' SEAT

2 DOOR BODY CELL WITH STANDARD FRONT AND VAN BACK

'unmechanical', being unable even to change a tyre. An artist-architect, he had little interest in the technical aspects of building. He drove an ordinary Ford Prefect, later changing to the more stylish BMW. Michael Hopkins collects vintage cars: he has three Alvises and a 1922 Sunbeam. For him, the appeal lies in seeing how everything works once you lift the bonnet. Among the cars owned by Eldred Evans of Evans and Shalev was a vintage Rolls-Royce: 'I had a string of vintage cars when I was a student, a 1750 Alfa, which was very fast, an Alvis with a pre-selector gearbox, a big Austin Six, lots of sports cars. At one stage I sold the Rolls and then bought it back. I couldn't really afford to run it.' Early in his career Piers Gough had a Jowett Javelin, later switching to an anonymous Honda Accord, but he said that what he really dreamt of owning was a Cadillac Eldorado – 'Very big, very flashy, with lots of chrome' – to complement his highly coloured postmodern architecture.

Marco Goldschmied from the Richard Rogers Partnership drove a 1973 Ferrari Dino GT, while Laurie Abbott of the same practice built his own car in 1981-82, having worked for Fiat with Renzo Piano. Only Daniel Libeskind rejected the motorcar, saying that, 'My attitude towards architecture is certainly free of the obsession with cars, their iconography and their perverse symbolism in modern architecture.' For Libeskind, too much emphasis on technology in architecture deprives it of cultural and spiritual qualities.

The *Building Design* article summed up the architect-automobile relationship by pointing out that cars are more than mere vehicles for getting from A to B: they have other values invested in them that make the choice very important in professional terms. Being aesthetes, designers, engineers and architects don't just choose the most expensive car on offer: they select their vehicle for looks, performance, design and to fit their approach to life.

Architecture and the Automobile

There can be no doubt that the development of both art and architecture in the early part of the twentieth century was influenced by the machine aesthetic. The universal use of machines in the form of automobiles, aircraft, trains and even domestic utensils had an impact on the shape and form of architectural elements. In 1955, Reyner Banham wrote that the machine aesthetic 'answered a clear cultural need in offering a common visual law, which united the form of the automobile and the building, which sheltered it.'[100] The machine concept introduced into architectural tasks notions of function and utility as well as engineering design, technological processes and new materials. Though some may disagree, it seems clear that this influence continues today with each technological advance, and will continue in the future.

Futurism, Constructivism and Functionalism

The first important group of artists and architects involved with the symbol of the automobile were the Futurists, as we have already seen. The whole essence of Futurist ideology was embodied in the automobile, the most tangible product and representation of contemporary technological revolution. Futurists saw reality in constant forward movement, which the car – the ambassador of new technology – symbolised perfectly. The painters Umberto Boccioni and Giacomo Balla used motorcars in their drawings, lithographs and paintings. Filippo Tommaso Marinetti, the founder of Futurism, celebrated the car in his writings and in the famous 'Futurist Manifesto'. Futurists realised that the car was affecting the environment, altering forever man's perception of the world. The car as machine, became an object that conveyed their ideals most clearly. 'The machine comes into Futurist poetics from an essentially aesthetic point of view. The machine is pleasing because it is beautiful and because being beautiful, it makes possible a new experience of poetry that is of life.'[101]

In his 1914 manifesto, Boccioni pointed the way forward for architecture, which the Futurists had until then ignored: 'In painting and sculpture, we have suppressed every superfluous decoration, every aesthetic preoccupation about the monumental, about the solemn and traditional. The general lines of cubes, pyramids and rectangles, including buildings, should be done away with, for they describe immobile architectural lines. All lines ought to be usable at any point and in any way. Through autonomy of component parts, buildings will stop being uniform, and will create architectural impressionism from which new possibilities for the future may be triggered. In fact, old and useless symmetry, always obtained at the expense of utility, will be destroyed. Just as with motorcars, a building's environment should perform to the maximum.'[102]

Antonio Sant'Elia, a Futurist architect, also published a manifesto in 1914 in which he proclaimed, 'We must invent and rebuild ex novo the modern city, like an immense and tumultuous building site – flexible, mobile, dynamic in its every part, and the modern house like a gigantic machine. The lifts must no longer be hidden away like tapeworms in the stairwells; but the stairs – which have become obsolete – must be abolished, and the lifts must clamber up facades like snakes of iron and glass. The house of concrete, iron and glass, without painted or sculpted decoration, rich only in the inherent beauty of its lines and modelling, will be extraordinarily brutal, ugly in its mechanical simplicity, its height and width determined by need – and not as municipal regulations prescribe.'[103] Sant'Elia compared the house to a machine years before Le Corbusier proposed the same idea in *Vers une architecture*. However, his was a more sinister, more masterful image than Corbusier's, which was expressed in purely functional terms.

The next artistic movement to become interested in the powerful imagery of the machine was Constructivism, which was founded in Moscow in 1920 by Naum Gabo and Antoine Pevsner when they issued their 'Realistic Manifesto'. Other artists who joined them included Vladimir Tatlin, Kasimir Malevich and El Lissitzky. Their aim was to make constructions in space using varied materials whose purpose was to express symbolically the concept of life and the study of the universe being supported by modern science and technology. All their objects had to be made efficiently to fulfil their purpose; new materials manufactured by modern industrial processes and the most modern methods of construction, providing the highest structural efficiency, were to be employed. Efficient machines – such as motorcars and aircraft – were cited as standards of excellence. The Constructivists did not attempt to design cars, but between 1931 and 1933 Vladimir Tatlin proposed a flying machine, which he called 'Letatlin', based on the same principles used by Leonardo da Vinci.

Functionalism, meanwhile, arose as the result of a number of inventions and innovations at the beginning of the twentieth century, which elevated the importance of the machine in the consciousness of artists and architects. The machine became a symbol of modern life, idolised and worshipped rather than regarded simply as an instrument for work or leisure. The Functionalists admired utilitarian, rational and logical forms and the structure of machines. They appreciated machine technology because in machines they saw the perfect example of functional elements assembled together, working efficiently and mass-produced as market forces demanded. Purist and functionalist architecture was clean, simple and white, its forms created in celebration and dramatisation of function. Its beauty was expressed by 'the promise of function'.[104] However, technology and function alone could not create good architecture or resolve the ideal form. The Functionalist approach subsequently gave rise in many cases to a sloppy, banal copying of standard Functionalist elements. It is only when technology is coupled with artistic invention that the successful resolution of a building's design can be reached.

The Bauhaus teachings encouraged young architectural students to include serious consideration of technology in their development of architectural skills. The very basis of the Bauhaus manifesto was contained in the proclamation, 'The ultimate aim of all creative activity is the building'; the original 1919 motto 'Art and craft, a new unity' changed after 1923 to 'Art and technology, a new unity'. The arts-and-technology syllabus helped Bauhaus students to become innovative avant-garde designers, able to discover new frontiers in their work.

Architecture and Mass-Production

By the 1920s machines, and especially cars, had become of such interest to artists and architects that a number of issues of *L'Esprit nouveau* were devoted purely to automobiles. Under the title 'Eyes Which Do Not See', issue number ten displayed some of the best French cars – Delage, Hispano-Suiza, Bignan-Sport, Bellanger, Voisin –

as if the magazine were a motor-show catalogue instead of an artistic publication. Issue number thirteen featured an article about prefabricated houses, illustrated not with a picture of a prefabricated house design, but with a photograph of the Bellanger saloon, showing its interior through an open door. The message was that for the construction of affordable prefabricated houses, industrial methods of production needed to be established on the same principles as those used in the factories of Ford and Citroën. As Le Corbusier wrote in *Vers une architecture*, 'If the problem of the dwelling or the flat were studied in the same way that a chassis is, a speedy transformation and improvement would be seen in our houses. If houses were constructed by industrial mass-production, like chassis, unexpected but sane and defensible forms would soon appear, and a new aesthetic would be formulated with astonishing precision.'[105]

Le Corbusier himself had Citroën cars in mind when he gave his prefabricated mass-produced house system the name 'Citrohan'. The source of his inspiration was a Citroën advertisement proclaiming, 'Citroën 10hp, the first French car in series production'. The Citrohan House (an idea first sketched out on the back of a menu in Le Mauroy restaurant, where Le Corbusier frequently dined) was shaped like a box with a large double-height living room and its upper bedroom floors set back to one side. Le Corbusier said it was 'Citrohan (not to say Citroën). That is to say, a house like a motorcar conceived and carried out like an omnibus or a ship's cabin.'[106]

André Citroën had visited Henry Ford in Detroit in the United States in 1912 to learn American assembly techniques and bring this knowledge back to Europe. (The American engineer Frederick Winslow Taylor, who died in 1915, had pioneered the scientific management of industrial production that revolutionised the country's approach to manufacture.) In the spring of 1913, Ford started to devise the first moving assembly line for the production of small parts; over the next year the lines were enlarged to include the whole production process for the Model T. By 1917, daily production was reaching 1,500 units. This kind of mass-production reduced the cost of products, making them affordable to a broader range of the public. Citroën started his production of the Model A on a moving-track assembly line with the first car becoming available in May 1919. Within a year, Citroën had produced 2,500 automobiles, beating all its French competitors. The Model A was a pleasant small car, popular with young people. The Citrohan House, shown in model form at the 1922 Salon d'automne, appeared as if it were made in the same factory from which the 10hp Citroën emerged. The house was like a saloon, not on wheels but, at least partly, on *pilotis*.

Frank Lloyd Wright's buildings were similarly affected by the forms produced by transport technology. Wright confirmed that the ocean liner, aeroplane and motorcar had influenced the architecture of his Larkin Administration Building in Buffalo, New York (built in 1904 and demolished in 1947). The building was 'a genuine expression of power directly applied to purpose'.[107] When Wright's Robie House was built on the corner of Woodlawn Avenue and East Fifty-Eighth Street in Chicago in 1909, it was perceived as having been inspired by a steamship. Its owner was Fred C Robie, the manufacturer of Excelsior bicycles and designer of an experimental car (1906-07) with a streamlined body on a 2.3-metre wheelbase fitted with an air-cooled, two-cylinder engine. The First World War prevented production of the car, which had been intended for the British market.

Herbert Johnson, Wright's client for the SC Johnson Wax Administration Building in Racine, Wisconsin (1936-39), was as keen on luxury cars as his architect and, like him, owned a Lincoln Zephyr, one of the most admired and successful streamlined American cars. It was speculated that the car's form could have inspired the streamlined architecture of the Johnson Wax Building, which was certainly not Wright's usual style. Wright claimed that he was the first to apply the term 'streamlining' to buildings, and was pleased when *Life* magazine observed that the building's interior looked 'like a woman swimming naked in a stream', responding that the Johnson Building was the feminine counterpart to the masculine Larkin Building.[108] Wright later wrote that: 'It was high time to give our hungry American public something truly "streamlined", so swift, sure of itself, and clean for its purpose ... that anybody could see the virtue of this thing called Modern ...'[109]

In 1925, Wright proposed for his client Gordon Strong a gigantic, spiral, double-lane ramp called 'The Automobile Objective', whose windowless interior accommodated a planetarium. Automobiles ascended and descended the ramp allowing passengers and drivers a bird's-eye view of the countryside. 'The Objective' was never built but Wright liked the ramp concept so much that he later used it in other projects – most successfully at the Solomon R Guggenheim Museum in New York (1943-59).

Architecture and Mobility

Wright saw the automobile as liberation. It allowed people to leave the crowded cities and live wherever they wanted to. 'By means of the motorcar and the collateral inventions that are here with it, the horizon of the individual has been immeasurably widened,' commented Wright.[110] His utopian Broadacre City concept, first published in 1932, developed this idea, choosing the best sites the cities and the countryside could offer and connecting them by means of the automobile. People who owned a car did not have to live crammed together in cities, reasoned Wright. Instead, they could spread into the landscape and live in harmony with nature. Each family unit would occupy an acre of land and all inner urban facilities would be integrated within a four-square-mile area. Crowded cities would be eliminated and people would work close to home. Driving along beautiful, efficient highways with safe, integrated lighting would be a pleasure. Traffic would occupy several levels of roads, with commercial vehicles, passenger cars and pedestrians each having their own dedicated routes. Wright described this arrangement: 'Great highways, safe in width and grade, bright with wayside flowers, cool with shade trees ... '[111] 'No need to get tangled up in spasmodic stop-and-go traffic in some wasteful stop-and-go trip to town nor to any "great" city as centre for everything whatever except to "view the ruins".'[112]

Wright supposed that each family would have at least one car, but of a much better design than those being produced in America at the time. 'The present form of the motorcar is crude and imitative compared with the varied forms of fleet machines, beautiful as such, manufacturers will soon be inclined or be soon compelled to make.'[113]

Unlike today's sterile suburban sprawl – which can be blamed in part on the spread of motorcar usage – the Broadacre City concept was designed to balance all the urban elements within a natural landscape setting in

Frank Lloyd Wright: Broadacre City, 1958. The image shows several versions of the Road Machine used here as taxi vehicles. (The Frank Lloyd Wright Foundation)

140

Bertrand Goldberg: Marina City,
Chicago, 1959-64, a good example of
the urban integration of home and car.
(from M Ragon, Goldberg, On the City,
Paris Art Centre, Paris, 1985)

which employment, schools, shopping and other services were all equally accessible from the home base.

The American avant-garde architect Bertrand Goldberg was also inspired by the mobility of the car, as can be seen in his designs for Marina City, Chicago (1959-64) and the innovative North Pole Ice Cream Store in River Forest, Illinois, built in 1938. Marina City consisted of two circular, sixty-five storey residential towers with car parking arranged on spiral ramps winding around the central cores in the lower twenty storeys of the buildings. The North Pole Ice Cream Store was devised as a trailer to be towed by a mother-truck and unfolded at its destination. The idea was that a number of these stores – square buildings suspended from masts – would be served by the mother-truck, where the ice cream would be manufactured. The stores were to be erected at parking areas in the north of the US during the summer and in the southern parts in winter.

Because of his Bauhaus training, Goldberg was concerned to combine German architectural economy with the American preoccupation with mass-production. He was interested in the prefabrication of steel furniture, bathrooms and kitchens. He designed prefabricated houses and, during the Second World War, devised armament containers that could be transformed into housing. In 1942, he proposed a mobile delousing unit, which used a truck body as a base element with a mast erected from it to support a tent structure fully surrounding the truck.

In the mid-1950s, the popular notion of mobility in architecture turned towards modular systems and the use of habitable cells. It was envisaged that these units would change their position from site to site and in horizontal and vertical planes. Urban areas were transcribed in complex, three-dimensional grids to establish an infrastructure for these modular cells. Automotive forms and technology inevitably influenced the resulting architecture. Ionel Schein, a Romanian architect living in France, was a pioneer of the architectural use of synthetic materials and the designer of the first all-plastic house, Maison en plastique (1955-56). His proposals for mobile hotel capsules (1956) and for a mobile library for Hachette using all-plastic materials were inspired by the architecture of automobile bodies.

The car and machines also figure prominently in the work of Alison and Peter Smithson, and clearly influenced their architectural designs. In their *Patio and Pavilion* exhibit created in collaboration with the photographer Nigel Henderson and sculptor Eduardo Paolozzi for the 'This is Tomorrow' exhibition in London in 1956, they constructed a habitat that included symbols for human needs: one was a wheel image to indicate movement and machines.

The Smithsons compared house and car design in an article entitled 'The Appliance House' in the April 1958 issue of *Architectural Design*. Their prefabricated Ideal Home House of the Future (1956), in which everything including appliances was fitted into allocated spaces, was designed – like a car – as a single entity, with a limited role. However, the Smithsons pointed out, an ordinary family house is not like a car: in a car very few things can be eliminated without destroying the performance of the whole; in an ordinary house there are many variables, and to remove or change some or many of them would not significantly alter performance. A house designed like a car is therefore at a disadvantage in some respects: with fittings so closely integrated into the structure,

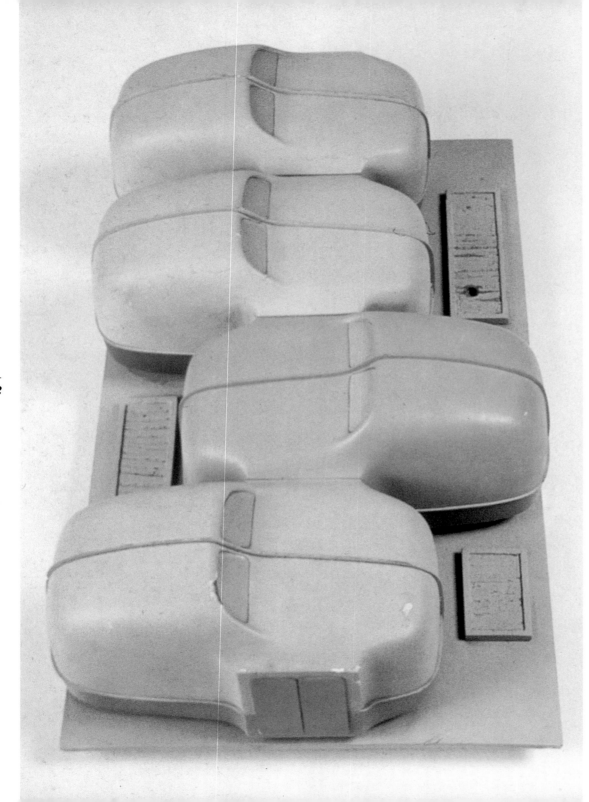

Ionel Schein: mobile library project, 1957, a direct transformation of an idea inspired by a car body into architecture. (Collection FRAC Centre, Orleans, photo P Magnon)

changing the refrigerator would be like trying to put a bigger glove compartment in a Volkswagen dashboard – it is easier to buy a new car.

The Smithsons' favourite car was the Citroën DS19, which inspired their handling of services and mechanical equipment in the Economist Building in London: '... ambient light, ambient air, no fuss about detail, awareness in a quiet way that the sweetness of functioning is architecture. In a large building it involves us with the organising of mechanicals and services with a clear formal objective in mind, for, as Louis Kahn said, the suspended ceiling speaks about nothing ... In a real building, the light and the space and the air are one. Sniff the air, sense the space, know how to act ... the answer seems to be ... light, on the whole, being made just to seem to be around; air arriving and departing obviously but unobtrusively; and the arrangement of the storage and work areas so that they indicate their intended use ... It would seem that one of the things that is crucial to large numbers and to repetition is a special sort of anonymity of styling.'[114]

In the mid-1960s, François Dallegret and Reyner Banham, a great automobile enthusiast, even proposed, when commenting on the American architectural tradition, that a building's servicing could be supplied or carried by a car: 'The car is already doing quite a lot of the standard-of-living package's job'. A simple, inflatable Mylar airdome over the mobile unit would provide the necessary weatherproof envelope. In this way, the 'house'

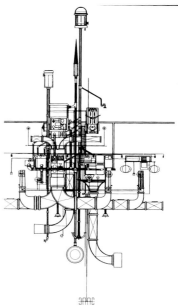

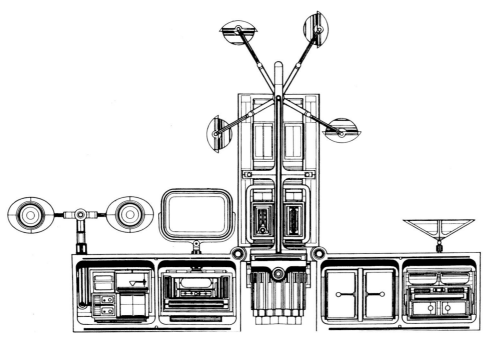

*François Dallegret: Anatomy of a Dwelling and Transportable Standard-of-Living package, 1965. Illustrations typify the 1960s obsession with man's accommodation combined with mobility. (*Art in America, *April 1965)*

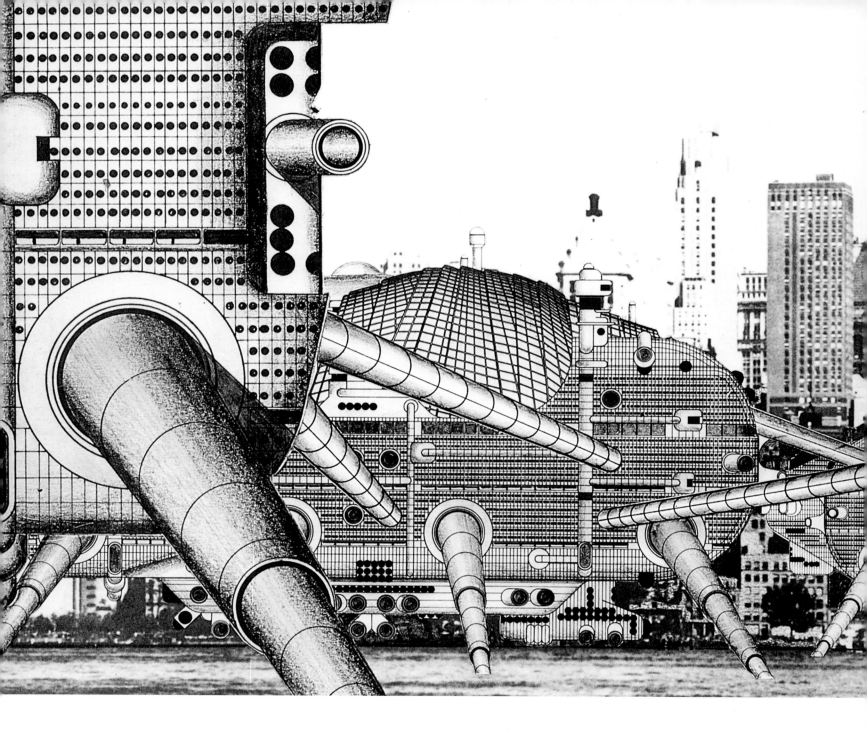

Ron Herron: Walking City in New York, 1964. (Archigram Archives, Dennis Crompton)

Michael Webb: Cushicle, 1966. Stage 1: chassis with unopened complete nomadic unit carried on man's back, 'a mechanism like a car'. (Archigram Archives, Dennis Crompton)

would become a service core set in infinite space. Banham saw no reason to employ solid monumental-space architecture in an open-fronted society, which had social and personal mobility, gadgetry and almost universal expendability.[115]

A few years earlier, a group of architectural students in London calling themselves Archigram had begun to put forward a vision of a future in which man and machines were even more closely intertwined. Founding a magazine (also called *Archigram*), they published experimental projects and questioned contemporary architecture. For them, the car became a symbol of an unadulterated era; unlike architecture, which was corrupted by its rigid traditions and its long history, the car had no historical connections or ties. Archigram's vision of the future was based on the symbiosis of man and machine, as seen in Michael Webb's Cushicle (1966) and Suitaloon (1968), and Ron Herron's Walking City (1964). Archigram's adoption of mobile technology based on the car's self-reliant mobility – seen, for example, in their Living Pod (1965) – and schemes such as Drive-in Housing (1964-66), Moment-Village (1967) and instant mobile cities, were a major influence on future architectural design, launching the second machine age and the high-tech architecture of the 1970s.

Architecture and Technology

The Archigram influence can be seen in Renzo Piano and Richard Rogers' competition-winning design for the Centre National d'Art et de Culture Georges Pompidou (1971-77) in Paris. According to Rogers, the Pompidou Centre was a giant Meccano set, 'a machine whose purpose was to create social interaction within the city'.[116] It was a machine that could respond fully to the urban environment and its inhabitants, spreading culture to the Parisian population and visitors; and it could alter its image, depending on what purpose it was being used for, and could communicate this to the outside world. With all its functions clearly visible and colour-coded, it was like a powerful car engine, revealed when the bonnet is lifted .

Norman Foster, who strives for innovation in all his projects, has long understood how architecture profits from the transfer of technologies from other industries. His design for the Hongkong and Shanghai Bank building (1979-86), for example, would not have been possible had he not been prepared to embrace expertise from aircraft, automobile and even bicycle technology. A number of components such as the honeycomb floor panels, the cantilevered brackets of the walkway and the plug-in service modules and handrails, drew on ideas from other technological spheres. The simple structure of his Nomos furniture system (1985-88) was based on the X-shaped backbone chassis of the Lotus Elan. The concept for the Sainsbury Centre (1974-77) at the University of East Anglia draws on the design of aircraft wings, with a smooth external cladding skin and an internal tuneable ceiling system of aluminium perforated louvres, in between which are contained all the necessary services, catwalks and control systems, including the structure.

One of Jan Kaplicky's dreams has been to use the monocoque construction techniques of the automobile, aviation and shipbuilding industries in his architecture. The earliest monocoque structure (sometimes known as 'integral-body', 'frameless construction' or, in the car industry, 'unit-construction body') was designed by the

Michael Webb: Suitaloon, 1968. Here the suit provides all the necessary services – clothing for living in. (Archigram Archives, Dennis Crompton)

marine engineer FW Hodges of the Vauxhall Iron Works in London, in 1903 for the first Vauxhall two-seater 5hp single-cylinder model. To save weight, Hodges transferred marine construction techniques (Vauxhall also manufactured marine engines at that time) to car structure by using sheet-metal body panels without a frame to support the whole vehicle.

Some years later, in 1912, the French aviation company Deperdussin made one of the first completely closed-body shell-type constructions. Deperdussin's monoplane fuselage was constructed of a cage-like wooden framework covered with stressed-skin plywood sheets. Other aircraft manufacturers soon followed suit, adopting lightweight metal instead of wood. The following year, the English automobile manufacturer, Lagonda, developed a two-seater car whose body structure consisted of two thin side rails, which supported the sheet body panels. In 1922, Lancia marketed its Lambda model, which had a body structure made of pressed sheet metal skeleton and panelling in a hull form.

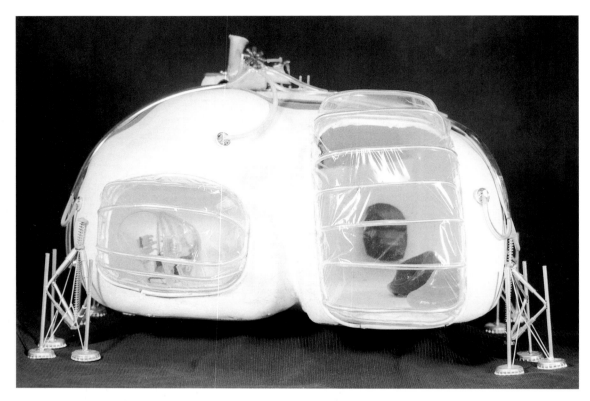

David Greene: Living Pod, 1965. Living accommodation with attached machines inspired by trailer homes. (Archigram Archives, Dennis Crompton)

However, the real advance in monocoque construction came with a patent submitted by Joseph Ledwinka, engineering director of the pioneering pressed-steel-sheet manufacturer, Budd Company, Philadelphia, in 1928. His intention was to manufacture frame and sheet panels separately and then assemble them into one complete unit; the independent frame was replaced by reinforced sections inside the body shell. Budd constructed a front-wheel-drive car prototype with a unit construction body and tried to persuade manufacturers such as Ford to adopt the new idea. Ford was unresponsive but André Citroën, who visited Budd in 1931, took the prototype drawings back to France and asked André Lefébvre, Flaminio Bertoni and Raoul Cuinet to design the Traction Avant Citroën 7CV, which was launched in 1934, using Budd's monocoque construction technique. Other automobile manufacturers, both in Europe and the US, slowly followed Citroën's example, and today, most car bodies are made of monocoque or semi-monocoque construction.

The use of monocoque construction techniques in architecture has certain advantages: it reduces the cost of

PLUG IN YOUR HOME NODE

HIGHLY SERVICED FREE TRAILER FRAME STAK-UP

FREE TIME NODE
TRAILER CAGE
RON HERRON-ARCHIGRAM

Ron Herron: Free Time Node Trailer Cage, 1967. Airstream
trailers providing instant drive-in-housing environment.
(Archigram Archives, Dennis Crompton)

*Lancia Lambda chassis and body
skeleton, 1922, one of the first
semi-monocoque car body
constructions.*

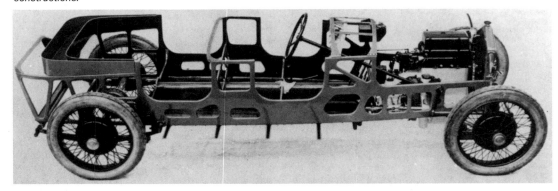

the separate frame by incorporating the necessary strength within the self-supporting building skin, which encloses the required structure-free internal space and keeps out the weather. However, a true monocoque construction – that is, a single skin such as an eggshell, a balloon skin or a GRP or aluminium-sheet small boat hull – is not strong enough to take the required loading and almost all techniques involve semi-monocoque constructions, which combine a structural skin and frame in one component.

Kaplicky used a semi-monocoque construction for his Media Centre project at Lord's Cricket Ground in London (1994-99) – the first example of this type of construction applied in architecture. The building's main shell body (manufactured by the Pendennis Shipyard in Falmouth) is raised on two concrete cores containing stairs and lifts. The shell is made of aluminium outer skin panels, 6 millimetres thick, which are welded on to 12-20 - millimetre-thick aluminium ribs. Each segment is approximately 4.5metres wide and 20 metres long. All twenty-six segments are assembled, bolted and fully welded together on site to create a seamless shell with internal ribbing. Internally, the shell is lined with a perforated, leatherette-type material (normally used to line car interiors and inspired by a 1957 pale blue Ford Thunderbird with streaks of white upholstery and chrome fittings) to provide acoustic conditions suitable for the purpose of the building.

Jan Kaplicky: NatWest Media Centre, Lord's Cricket Ground, London, 1994-99, the first semi-monocoque building structure in the world. Soon after its opening, the building's image was used for a television commercial advertising the new Rover 75. (Richard Davies)

Architecture and Prefabrication

Another, more fundamental, notion that architecture took from automobile production was prefabrication. The beautiful form of the Airstream trailer designed by Wally Byam in 1935 inspired Ron Herron of Archigram to propose the Trailer Cage (1967), a highly serviced frame structure in which the trailers were 'plugged in' on several levels as 'home nodes'. In 1970, the American architect Paul Rudolph, who nicknamed the trailer 'the twentieth-century brick', designed and built the Oriental Masonic Gardens in New Haven to provide low-cost housing, assembling 12-foot-wide mobile home units to create 148 modules of two- to five-bedroom apartments.

While acting as consultant at the Ministry of Works in 1949, Joseph Emberton, who liked fast cars, proposed a prototype for a prefabricated steel house. This adopted automobile construction methods using load-bearing, pressed-steel, outer skin panels filled with aerated concrete. The roof panels were similar, but curved to gain extra stiffness. Each house would have taken eleven men one week to erect. The prototype house was built by a motorcar-body manufacturer, Briggs Bodies, Dagenham, Essex. However, the shortage of steel prevented further development.

While designing the Unité d'habitation in Marseilles (1945-52), Le Corbusier hit upon a new idea for the construction of apartment buildings, though he did not use it in Marseilles. 'We have taken a momentous step, introducing an entirely new concept in the theory of housing – and into its practice. The dwelling is regarded as a thing in itself. It contains a family. A thing in itself, with its own reality, its own criteria, its own requirements. It's a bottle. And, having made our bottle, the dwelling, we can plump it down under an apple tree in Normandy or under a pine tree in the Jura. We can equally well shove it in a pigeonhole, that is to say into a space on the fifth or seventeenth floor of a steel framework. It won't make any difference to the thing in itself or to the way we make it. Yes, we can put it anywhere we like in what might be called the supporting skeleton. Or more simply, a wine-bin. We just stow the bottle away in the bin.'[117] With this idea, Le Corbusier was reinforcing the notion of the prefabricated pod (now commonly considered for bathroom construction) already suggested by Buckminster Fuller in 1936.

However, because of the demand for individuality, architects' attempts to introduce the standardisation of building components or even whole buildings have been largely unsuccessful over the years. People want to project their personality onto all their possessions, and onto their homes in particular. Moreover, the uniformly created buildings that result from total prefabrication and standardisation go against the architect's natural creativity. The sight of caravan holiday parks, the most common example of prefabricated accommodation, or housing estates constructed in prefabricated panel systems, are deplored for being soulless. What is needed is the correct balance of prefabrication and purpose-designed elements.

One of the greatest challenges facing architects interested in industrialisation is breaking the conservative attitude of the building construction industry, which resists all innovation and stubbornly persists in using obsolete traditional methods. To educate contractors in the higher art of factory- or mass-production has been a long process. The building construction operation is labour intensive and therefore expensive, slow and error-prone, and yet other working methods have rarely been tried. Until architects can persuade the whole building team to adopt their vision of industrialised machine production, architecture will have a hard time transforming itself into a totally modern enterprise.

'Automobiles as the manifestation of a complex and agitated culture-within-a-culture producing discrete objects, which are themselves environments for human activities, provide a standard of comparison for the activities of the architectural profession', wrote Reyner Banham in 1960. '[Architects] may ruefully compare the scale of the constructional work produced by the automobile culture with that entrusted to architects; they may enviously admire the apparently close communion that exists between users and producers, the direct way in which designers and stylists seem to be able to apprehend the needs of motorists and satisfy them.'[118]

Architects, by contrast, tend to have little contact with the man in the street and little experience of designing for or dealing with the public at large – a fact that becomes obvious whenever public discussions are instigated about the design of important new public buildings. Architecture should learn not only from car body styling (which often succumbs to prevailing fashions) but also from body construction techniques, which transcend vogues and short-lived trends. Automobile construction technology indicates new ways of structuring and detailing components, which could be easily transferred to building technology. Reyner Banham celebrated the architect who seeks to keep pace with progress in technology and who realises that he will have to be in 'fast company'. In order to keep up, wrote Banham, he may have to emulate the Futurists and discard his whole cultural load. 'If, on the other hand, he decides not to do this, he may find that a technological culture has decided to go on without him.'[119]

The Way Ahead

The important point about automobile manufacture is that it constantly forges forward. Car manufacturers must keep their research and development programmes running in order to bring out new or updated models every year, with improved fuel consumption, better engines requiring less maintenance, a longer life, more gadgets and more safety features. Mass-produced cars will never return to the days of their humble beginnings (except for the nostalgic body reproductions recently attempted in Japan and by kit-car manufacturers), unlike architecture, which continuously and apologetically looks back over its shoulder.

In his collection of lectures published under the title *Art and Technics*, the American architectural critic Lewis Mumford pointed the way for architects to practise with a clear conscience: 'The need for expression remains a constant in every culture; without it the drama of life cannot go on, and the plot itself becomes pointless and empty. Life must have meaning, value, and purpose, or we die: we die standing on our feet, with our eyes open, but blind, our ears open but deaf, our lips moving but speechless. And we cannot, by any mechanical duplication of old symbols, come to a realisation of the vital meanings in our own life. Our intercourse with other ages can only be of a spiritual nature. Everything we take over from the past must disappear in the act of digestion and assimilation, to be transformed into our own flesh and bones. Each age then must live its own life.'[120]

The twenty-first century will be confronted with the task of completing the projects that the twentieth century has, perhaps somewhat hastily, set in motion. The use of cars will have to be fully justified and all vehicles will need to be designed with even greater care for safety and the environment. Automatic road-guidance systems will be established, and computers will be programmed to help drive our vehicles. New engines will be adopted, based on fuel-cell technology and consuming fuels without harming the atmosphere. Communications technology will continue to dazzle us with its astonishing new achievements. Architecture will need to look closely at developments in art and technology, and it must make use of new materials, new skills, new attitudes and new construction methods if it is to keep pace with the new age. Those architects who want to be involved with the new will keep on sketching machines that can help people enjoy their lives. However, the progress of technology must not overrun the basic human aspirations; it must not thwart our quest for individuality, self-expression and adventure, nor limit our pursuit of liberty, tolerance, happiness, fun and love.

Notes

1 The vast majority of the repetitive forms of housing estates are creations instigated by building construction firms using standard designs, as opposed to each house being individually commissioned from architectural firms As such, they have nothing to do with 'architecture'

2 Martin Pawley, *Theory and Design in the Second Machine Age*, Basil Blackwell, Oxford, 1990, p59

3 Walter Gropius, 'autostandard und künstlerische gestaltung' (1932), republished in *Form + Zweck*, issue 2, Berlin, 1983, pp13-14

4 Arthur Drexler, *Ten Automobiles*, exhibition catalogue, The Museum of Modern Art, New York, September 1953, p2

5 Ibid, p3

6 Stephen Bayley, 'Grace ... Pace ... Space', *The Architectural Review*, London, November 1984, p77

7 Le Corbusier, *Œuvre complète*, Part 3, 1934-38, Editions Girsberger, Zurich, 1939, p24

8 Theo van Doesburg, 'Misunderstanding Cubist Principles in Czechoslovakia and Elsewhere', *Het Bouwbedrijf*, vol.3, no.10, The Hague, September 1926, pp346-9

9 Le Corbusier in collaboration with Amédée Ozenfant, 'Les maisons "Voisin"', *L'Esprit nouveau*, no 2, Paris, 1920, pp211-4

10 See B Bruce-Briggs, *The War Against the Automobile*, EP Dutton, New York , 1977, p81

11 Jules Verne, *La maison à vapeur*, 1880, quoted in Gerald Silk, *Automobile and Culture*, Abrams, New York, 1984, p40

12 Stephen Bayley, *In Good Shape*, The Design Council, London, 1979, p11

13 Guillaume Apollinaire, 'La Petite Auto', quoted in Silk, *Automobile and Culture*, p57

14 Filippo Tommaso Marinetti, 'Futurist Manifesto', *Le Figaro*, Paris, 20 February 1909

15 Umberto Boccioni, 'Architettura futurista manifesto' (1914; first published in 1972), reprinted in *Architectural Design*, nos 1-2, London, 1981, p17

16 Picabia collaborated on this Surrealist film of 1924 with Marcel Duchamp; it was directed by René Clair

17 Jennifer Gough-Cooper and Jacques Caumont, *Ephemerides on and about Marcel Duchamp and Rrose Sélavy 1887-1968*, Thames & Hudson, London, 1993, no pagination, see October 1912

18 Paul Haviland, *291* magazine, New York, Autumn 1915, quoted in Silk, *Automobile and Culture*, p79

19 Joris-Karl Huysmans, Là-Bas, 1891, quoted in Robert Hughes, *The Shock of the New*, Thames & Hudson, London, 1991, p51

20 Filippo Tommaso Marinetti, 'To the Automobile', 1905, quoted in Silk, *Automobile and Culture,* p67

21 John Steinbeck, *Cannery Row* (1945), quoted from edition Arrow, London, 1995, pp55-6

22 Roland Barthes, 'The New Citroën', *Mythologies* (1957), republished in English by Vintage, London, 1993, p89

23 Ibid

24 Richard Hamilton, *Collected Words 1952-82*, Thames & Hudson, London, 1982, p19

25 See Alan Windsor, *Peter Behrens*, The Architectural Press, London, 1981, p23

26 See Joseph-August Lux, *Ingenieur-Aesthetik*, Verlag von Gustav Lammers, 1910, pp50-56; quoted in Stephen Bayley, *In Good Shape*, pp25-28

27 Fernand Léger, 'The Machine Aesthetic', *Bulletin de l'Effort Moderne*, Paris, January-February 1924, reprinted in Fernand Léger, *Functions of Painting*, Thames & Hudson, London, 1973, pp52-61

28 See Herbert Read, *Art and Industry* (1934), Faber & Faber, London, third edition, 1953, pp54-55

29 Raymond Loewy, *La laideur se vend mal*, Gallimard, Paris, 1995, p282

30 Reyner Banham, 'Machine Aesthetics', *The Architectural Review*, London, April 1955, pp225-28

31 Later collected and published by Le Corbusier in *Vers une architecture*, Editions Georges Crés et çie, Paris, 1923. This was translated into English

by Frederick Etchells and published as *Towards a New Architecture* by Rodker, London, in 1927

32 Norman Bel Geddes, *Horizons*, Dover, New York, 1977, second edition, pp19-20

33 Norman Foster, 'Boeing 747', *Building Sights*, BBC Television, 1991

34 Le Corbusier, *Towards a New Architecture*, Rodker, London, 1931, pp.110-11

35 Ibid., p109

36 Jaromír Kejcar, 'The Architecture of Transatlantic Liners', *Zivot II*, Prague, 1922, p 38

37 William R Lethaby, *Form in Civilisation* (1920), quoted in FRS Yorke, *The Modern House in England*, The Architectural Press, London, 1947, p7

38 FRS Yorke, *The Modern House*, The Architectural Press, London, 1951, p.18

39 Museum of Modern Art, New York, press release (no 510823-46), 1951

40 Emily Genauer, 'Cars at Museum', *New York Herald Tribune*, 20 September 1953

41 'Boxes and Envelopes', *The New Yorker*, New York, 3 October 1953

42 Gino Severini, 'Machinery', *De Stijl*, Leiden, vol 5, no 12, 1922, quoted from Tim and Charlotte Benton, with Dennis Sharp, *Form Follows Function*, The Open University Press, London, 1975, p96

43 Norman Foster, speech given on occasion of the Solar Electric Vehicle launch, Royal Botanic Gardens, Kew, London, 28 September 1994

44 There are many publications devoted to the life and work of Le Corbusier, but they are inconsistent when discussing his Voisin car: 8hp, 10hp, 13hp and 14hp models are mentioned. However, the Les Amis de Gabriel Voisin club confirmed that Le Corbusier's car was the 10hp model

45 Le Corbusier, *Œuvre complète*, Part 2, 1929-34, first published in Zurich, 1935; quoted from the 1964 edition, p202

46 Photographs of later projects, such as the Cité de Refuge of 1929-33 in Paris, show the six-cylinder type, C11, 14hp Voisin, though there is no proof that Le Corbusier ever owned this car, which may have been borrowed for the occasion

47 Le Corbusier, *Almanach d'architecture moderne*, Paris, 1925, p195

48 Vladimir Karfík, *Architekt si spomína*, Spolok Architektov Slovenska, Bratislava, 1993, p72

49 Ibid

50 Ibid., p 59

51 See Peter Blake, *The Master Builders*, WW Norton & Co, New York, 1976, pp24-5

52 Robert Venturi, *Complexity and Contradiction in Architecture*, Museum of Modern Art, New York, 1977, p42

53 Jan Kaplicky, *For Inspiration Only*, Academy Editions, London, 1996

54 John Wright, *My Father Who is on Earth*, Putman, New York, 1946, quoted in 'Frank Lloyd Wright's Automobiles', *Frank Lloyd Wright Quarterly*, Scottsdale, Spring 1997, vol 8, no 2, p9

55 Frank Lloyd Wright, *An Autobiography*, Quartet, London, 1979, pp.436-37

56 Ben Masselink, 'The Glamour of a Red Convertible', *Frank Lloyd Wright Quarterly*, op. cit., p13

57 Frank Lloyd Wright, quoting KA Timiriazev, *Architectural Forum*, 68, New York, January 1938, p102

58 Quoted in 'Frank Lloyd Wright's Automobiles', *Frank Lloyd Wright Quarterly*, op. cit., p9

59 Karfík, *Architekt si spomína*, p38

60 See also Amédée Ozenfant, *Foundations of Modern Art*, Dover, New York, 1952, p152

61 See Tim Benton, *The Villas of Le Corbusier 1920-1930*, Yale University Press, London, 1987, p81

62 Karel Honzík, *Ze zivota avantgardy*, Ceskoslovensky spisovatel, Prague 1963, p126

63 Richard Etlin, 'A Paradoxical Avant-Garde, Le Corbusier's Villas of the 1920s', *The Architectural Review*, London, January 1987, p31

64 Fondation Le Corbusier, Paris, archive inventory numbers 23001, 22988, 23001, 22988 respectively

65 Frederick Usher and Griffith Borgeson, 'Corby – An Architect and His Maximum-Car', *Automobile Quarterly*, vol XVI, no 2, Princeton, Second Quarter 1978, pp208-9

66 Lisa L Ponti, *Gio Ponti, The Complete Work 1923-78*, Thames & Hudson, London, 1990, p167

67 Ibid

68 Ibid

69 Thomas Hines, *Richard Neutra and the Search for Modern Architecture*, Oxford University Press, New York, 1982, p99

70 Ibid

71 Norman Bel Geddes, letter to M Chapman, 22 March 1946; quoted from Arthur J Pulos, 'Design Horizons', *Rassegna* 60, Milan, p15

72 Bel Geddes, *Horizons*, p26

73 Paul Jaray, 'The Falling Drop, Not a "Teardrop"!', *Deutsche-Motor-Zeitschrift*, no 5/6, 1924

74 Dennis Sharp, 'Buckminster Fuller: A Tribute', *The Architect's Journal*, 14 December 1995, p20

75 Quoted from Richard Buckminster Fuller Chronofile, James Meller, *The Buckminster Fuller: Reader,* Jonathan Cape, London 1970, p14

76 Buckminster Fuller, *Autobiographical Monologue*, ed R Snyder, St Martin's Press, New York, 1980, p71

77 Quoted from Martin Pawley, 'The Car That Never Flew', *Blueprint*, London, September 1989, p50

78 In 1933, the Ford engine power was increased to 75bhp by raising the compression ratio and fitting aluminium cylinder heads; in 1934 it was increased to 90bhp thanks to the introduction of a duplex carburettor. In his *Autobiographical Monologue*, Buckminster Fuller mentions that Henry Ford gave him a 70 per cent discount on all the equipment he needed and that the V8 engine was then brand new. One can therefore assume that it was the 1932 65bhp version rather than 90bhp quoted by Buckminster Fuller

79 Buckminster Fuller, *Autobiographical Monologue*, p75

80 Ibid., p77

81 Christopher Morley, *Streamlines*, Doubleday, Doran & Co, New York, 1936

82 Norman Foster, 'Insights That Last Forever', *The Architect's Journal*, London, 14 December 1995, p26

83 See Giuseppe Pagano, *Architectural Design*, nos 1-2, London, 1981, p58

84 Werner Graeff, 'On the Form of the Motorcar', *Die Form*, I, Berlin, 1925-26, pp195-201; quoted in Tim and Charlotte Benton, with Dennis Sharp, *Form Follows Function*, Open University Press, London, 1975, p222

85 Ibid

86 *Jean Prouvé, Cours du CNAM 1957-70*, Pierre Mardaga, Liège, 1990, frontispiece

87 Ibid., p250

88 François Chaslin, 'The Great Tinsmith Jean Prouvé', *Rassegna* 14, Milan, 1983, p60.

89 See *1972-1982 Bericht einer deutschen unternehmung*, exhibition catalogue, Alexander Verlag, Berlin, 1983, p27

90 See *The Cantilever Chair*, exhibition catalogue Alexander Verlag, Berlin, 1986, p90

91 David Hodges, *The Le Mans 24-Hour Race*, Temple Press Books, London, 1963, pp71, 111

92 Norman Foster, *Sketches*, Birkhäuser Verlag, Basel, 1992, p25

93 Steve Braidwood, 'Carchitecture: Fiat's New Approach', *Design*, London, August 1982, p32

94 Massimo Dini, *Renzo Piano,* Electa, Milan, 1983, p38

95 Braidwood, 'Carchitecture', p33

96 Erich Mendelsohn, *Das Gesamtschaffen des Architekten*, Berlin, 1930, pp23-24ff

97 Sherban Cantacuzino, *Wells Coates, A Monograph*, Gordon Fraser, London, 1978, p17

98 Alan Thompson, 'What's Yours Called?', *Building Design*, London, 13 March 1987, pp14-20

99 Giles Worsley, 'Driving It Home', *Weekend Financial Times Magazine*, London, 4 April 1998, pp45-50

100 Reyner Banham, 'Machine Aesthetics', *The Architectural Review*, London, April 1955, p229

101 Alberto Asor Rosa, 'La cultura', *Storia d'Italia*, Einaudi, Turin, 1975, IV, p1296

102 Umberto Boccioni, 'Manifesto' (1914), *Architectural Design*, nos 1-2, London, 1981, p18

103 Antonio Sant'Elia, 'Manifesto 1914, published in *Architectural Design*, nos 1-2, London, 1981, pp20-1

104 Lewis Mumford, *Art and Technics*, Oxford University Press, London, 1952, p117; Mumford quotes Horatio Greenough

105 Le Corbusier, *Towards a New Architecture*, p133

106 Ibid., p240

107 Frank Lloyd Wright, *An Autobiography*, Quartet, London, 1979, p175

108 Brendan Gill, *Many Masks*, Heinemann, London, 1990, p371

109 Lloyd Wright, *An Autobiography*, p471

110 Lloyd Wright, *The Disappearing City* (1932), in *Frank Lloyd Wright Collected Writings*, vol 3 1931-39, Rizzoli, New York, 1993, p85

111 Ibid., p91

112 Lloyd Wright, *An Autobiography*, 1979, p354

113 Lloyd Wright, *The Disappearing City*, vol 3, 1931-39, p91

114 Peter Smithson, 'Concealment and Display', *Architectural Design*, London, July 1966, quoted in Alison and Peter Smithson, *Changing the Art of Inhabitation*, Artemis, London, 1994, p123

115 See Reyner Banham, 'A Home is Not a House', *Art in America*, New York, April 1965, reprinted in Reyner Banham, *Design by Choice*, Academy Editions, London, 1981, pp56-60

116 Deyan Sudjic, *Rogers, Foster, Sterling*, Thames & Hudson, London, 1986, p52

117 Le Corbusier, *The Marseilles Block*, Harvill Press, London, 1953, pp42-44

118 Banham, 'Stocktaking', *The Architectural Review*, London, February 1960, reprinted in Reyner Banham, *Design by Choice*, pp52-53

119 Banham, *Theory and Design in the First Machine Age*, Butterworth-Heinemann, London, 1960, p330

120 Mumford, *Art and Technics*, p123

Select Bibliography

Articles and Magazines:

Banham, Reyner, 'Machine Aesthetics', *The Architectural Review*, London, April 1955

Bayley, Stephen, 'Grace ... Pace ... Space', *The Architectural Review*, November 1984, p77

Chaslin, François, 'The Great Tinsmith Jean Prouvé', *Rassegna* 14, Milan, 1983

Doesburg, Theo van, 'Misunderstanding Cubist Principles in Czechoslovakia and Elsewhere', *Het Bouwbedrijf*, vol 3, no 10, The Hague, September 1926, pp346-9

Etlin, Richard A, 'A Paradoxical Avant-Garde, Le Corbusier's Villas of the 1920s', *The Architectural Review*, London, January 1987

Foster, Norman, 'Insights That Last Forever', *The Architect's Journal*, London, 14 December 1995

Frank Lloyd Wright Quarterly, vol 8, no 2, Scottsdale, Spring 1997

Glancey, Jonathan, 'Citroën 2CV', *The Architect's Journal*, London, 13 August 1986

Margolius, Ivan, 'Streamliners', *World Architecture*, no 39, 1995

Rassegna, nos 14, 18, 60, Milan

Thompson, Alan, 'What's Yours Called', *Building Design*, London, 13 March 198.

Worsley, Giles, 'Driving It Home', *Weekend Financial Times Magazine*, London, 4 April 1998

Books:

Banham, Reyner, *Design by Choice*, Academy Editions, London, 1981

Banham, Reyner, *Theory and Design in the First Machine Age*, Butterworth-Heinemann, London, 1960

Barker, Ronald and Harding, Anthony, *Automobile Design*, David & Charles, Newton Abbot, 1970

Bayley, Stephen, *In Good Shape*, The Design Council, London, 1979

Bayley, Stephen, *Sex, Drink and Fast Cars*, Pantheon Books, New York, 1986

Bayley, Stephen, *Taste*, The Conran Foundation, London, 1983

Bel Geddes, Norman, *Horizons*, Dover, New York, 1977, second edition

Benton, Tim and Charlotte with Sharp, Dennis, *Form Follows Function*, The Open University Press, London, 1975

Benton, Tim, *The Villas of Le Corbusier 1920-1930*, Yale University Press, London, 1987

Boyne, Walter J, *Power Behind the Wheel*, Conran Octopus, London, 1988

Brino, Giovanni, *Carlo Mollino*, Thames & Hudson, London, 1987

Cook, Peter, *Archigram*, Birkhäuser Verlag, Basel, 1991

Courteault, Pascal, *Automobiles Voisin 1919-1958*, White Mouse Editions, London 1991

Dini, Massimo, *Renzo Piano*, Electa, Milan, 1983

Dunas, Peter, *Luigi Colani*, Prestel Verlag, Munich, 1993

Foster, Norman, *Sketches*, Birkhäuser Verlag, Basel, 1992

Gill, Brendan, *Many Masks*, Heinemann, London, 1990

Heskett, John, *Industrial Design*, Thames & Hudson, London, 1980

Hines, Thomas, *Richard Neutra and the Search for Modern Architecture*, Oxford University Press, New York, 1982

Honzík, Karel, *Ze zivota avantgardy*, Ceskolovensky spisovatel, Prague, 1963

Hughes, Robert, *The Shock of the New*, Thames & Hudson, London, 1991

Hultén, Pontus K G, *The Machine*, MoMA, New York, 1968

Isaacs, Reginald, *Walter Gropius*, Little, Brown & Co, Boston, 1991

Jenger, Jean, *Le Corbusier Architect of a New Age*, Thames & Hudson, London, 1996

Jennings, Jan, *Roadside America, The Automobile in Design and Culture*, Iowa State University Press, Ames, 1990

Kaplicky, Jan, *For Inspiration Only*, Academy Editions, London, 1996

Karfík, Vladimír, *Architekt si spomína*, Spolok Architektov Slovenska, Bratislava, 1993

Lambot, Ian, *Norman Foster Buildings and Projects*, vol 3, Watermark, Hong Kong, 1989

Le Corbusier, *Aircraft*, The Studio, London, 1935

Le Corbusier, *Precisions*, MIT Press, Cambridge Massachusetts,1991

Le Corbusier, *Towards a New Architecture*, Rodker, London, 1931

Lichtenstein, Claude and Engler, Franz, *Streamlined, A Metaphor for Progress*, Lars Müller, Baden, 1996

Mclellan, John, *Bodies Beautiful*, David & Charles, Newton Abbot, 1975

Mumford, Lewis, *Art and Technics*, Oxford University Press, London, 1952

Ozenfant, Amédée, *Foundations of Modern Art*, Dover, New York, 1952

Pawley, Martin, *Buckminster Fuller*, Trefoil, London, 1990

Pawley, Martin, *Future Systems*, London, 1993

Pawley, Martin, *Hauer-King House*, London, 1996

Pawley, Martin, *Theory and Design in the Second Machine Age*, Basil Blackwell, Oxford, 1990

Penh, Wolfgang, *Die Erfindung der geschichte*, Prestel Verlag, Munich, 1989

Ragon, Michael, *Goldberg, On the City*, Paris Art, Paris, 1985

Read, Herbert, *Art and Industry*, Faber & Faber, London, 1953

Rice, Peter, *An Engineer Imagines*, Ellipsis, London, 1996

Rukschcio, Burkhardt, and Schachel, Roland, *Adolf Loos*, Rezidenz Verlag, Salzburg, 1982

Sekler, Eduard F, *Josef Hoffmann*, Princeton University Press, Princeton, 1985

Setright, LJ K, *The Designers*, Weidenfeld and Nicholson, London, 1976

Silk, Gerald, *Automobile and Culture*, Abrams, New York, 1984

Smithson, Peter and Alison, *The 1930s*, Alexander Verlag, Berlin, 1985

Smithson, Peter and Alison, *Changing the Art of Inhabitation*, Artemis, London, 1994

Steegmuller, Francis, *Appolinaire*, Rupert Hart-Davis, London, 1963

Sudjic, Deyan, *Cult Objects*, Paladin, London, 1985

Sudjic, Deyan, *Rogers, Foster, Sterling*, Thames & Hudson, London, 1986

Teague, Walter D, *Design This Day*, The Studio, London, 1946

Tubbs, DB, *Art and the Automobile*, Chartwell Books, Secaucus, 1989

Wallis, Alan D, *Wheel Estate*, The John Hopkins University Press, Baltimore, 1997

Wright, Frank Lloyd Wright, *An Autobiography*, Quartet, London 1979

Yorke, FRS, *The Modern House*, The Architectural Press, London 1951

Acknowledgements

This is a complex book and in its preparation a number of friends helped formulate my ideas. In 1990, John G Henry and I had started to discuss, research and collect material. Jan Kaplicky and Colin Rose advised throughout the time of writing, suggesting further subjects. Mandy Bates and Heda Margolius Kováły reread the manuscript several times, making valuable comments. Rachel Bean and Jane Lamacraft skilfully edited the flow of the text. Dr Philippe Ladure of Les Amis de Gabriel Voisin clarified the difficult model classification and identification of Le Corbusier's car. Sylvie Paquet helped with French translations and research. Foster and Partners allowed me time off work to concentrate on writing. Maggie Toy enthusiastically accepted the book for publication. Corinne Masciocchi and Abigail Grater endeavoured to find all the necessary illustrations from various foundations, institutions, museums and libraries. Mariangela Palazzi-Williams finally took on the task of getting the book into print. Without the help of all those involved, this publication would not be on your bookshelf.

Index

Abbott, Laurie 133
Adam, Robert 130
Alen, William van 130
Ambasz, Emilio 123
Andreau, Jean Edouard 59
Apollinaire, Guillaume 13
Archigram 146, 152
Architectural Association 23, 59
Arp, Jean 127
Auriol, Vincent 50
Avery, Bryan 131, 132

Bacon, Roger 11
Balla, Giacomo 134
Banham, Reyner 20, 22, 54, 134, 143, 146, 153
Barberis, Charles 121
Barthes, Roland 16, 18
Bayley, Stephen 7
Becchia, Walter 50
Behrens, Peter 18
Bel Geddes, Norman 10, 22, 67-69, 70-74, 81
Bellini, Mario 119, 120
Benz, Karl 12
Berlage, Hendrik Petrus 112
Bertoni, Flaminio 16, 28, 48, 50, 53, 122, 127, 148
Bierbaum, Otto Julius 26
Bill, Max 26
Blake, Peter 31
Boccioni, Umberto 13, 14, 134
Boulanger, Pierre-Jules 16, 48, 49, 50-52
Brancusi, Constantin 127
Breer, Carl 81
Bremner, Craig 106
Breuer, Marcel 90, 91
Broadley, Eric 127
Broglie, Maurice 48
Brumwell, Marcus 127
Buckminster Fuller, Richard 75-79, 80-83
Buffet, Gabrielle 15
Bugatti, Ettore 54
Burgess, Starling 77
Burton, Decimus 101
Byam, Wally 152

Cadiou, Jean 50
Calder, Alexander 123
Campo, Franco 95
Camus, Albert 16
Capek, Josef and Karel 102

Carney, Richard 38
Casson, Hugh 130
Chapman, John 32
Chaslin, François 89
Citroën, André 48, 136, 148
Claveau, Emile 59
Coates, Wells 128, 129
Colani, Luigi 127
Cugnot, Nicolaus-Joseph 12
Cuinet, Raoul 148
Curtiss, Glenn 106

Daimler, Gottlieb 12
Dallegret, François 143
Dalmonte, Mario 92, 94-96
Davies, David 131
Dean, James 16
Derain, André 26
Design Research Associates Limited 7
Design Research Unit 127
Diana, Princess 16
Dixon, Fenella 130
Döblin, Alfred 26
Doesburg, Theo van 7
Doren, van Harold 10
Drexler, Arthur 6, 25
Dreyfuss, Henry 10
Duchamp, Marcel 15
Duncan, Ronald Aver 59, 60

'Eight Automobiles' 24
Emberton, Joseph 60, 61, 152
Epstein, Jacob 25
Evans, Eldred 133
Evans, Oliver 12

Farman, Henry 54
Fayed, Dodi 16
Feuchtwanger, Leon 26
Fiorucci, Elio 120
Fletcher, Bannister 130
Forceau, Alphonse 48
Ford, Edsel 33, 36
Ford, Henry 36, 77, 136
Fornaroli, Antonio 28
Foster, Norman 23, 83, 97-99, 100, 101, 131, 146
Frugés, Henri 54

Gabo, Naum 127, 135
Gallimard, Michel 16

Gehry, Frank 130
Genauer, Emily 25
Giacosa, Dante 59
Goldberg, Bertrand 102, 117, 140, 141
Goldschmied, Marco 133
Gough, Piers 133
Gowing, Lawrence 18
Graeff, Werner 86, 87
Graffi, Carlo 95
Graham, Ray 72
Greene, David 148
Grégoire, J A 59
Gregr, Vladimír 118
Gropius, Walter 6, 43-48

Hamilton, Richard 18
Hansom, Joseph Aloysius 11, 32
Haviland, Paul 15
Henderson, Nigel 141
Herron, Ron 144-146, 149, 152
Hodges, F W 147
Hoffmann, Josef 11, 62
Honzík, Karel 55
Hopkins, Michael 133
Hume, Fergus 32
Hutchinson, Max 131
Huysmans, Joris-Karl 15

Jankovits, Gino and Oscar 116
Jaray, Paul 72, 80, 81
Jeanneret, Pierre 57
Jiricná, Eva 102, 130
Johnson, Herbert 137
Johnson, Homer H 65
Johnson, Philip 24, 25, 65
Junkers aircraft 49, 90

Kahn, Louis 143
Kaiser, Henry J 82
Kaplicky, Jan 31, 102-106, 146, 150, 151
Kardous, Frantisek 118
Karfík, Vladimír 30, 42
Keck, Fred 80
Kelly, Grace 16
Khahn, Quasar 123
Kleyer, Heinrich 44, 90
Kotera, Jan 112
Krejcar, Jaromír 23

Lamborghini, Ferruccio 130

Lancia, Vincenzo 42
Le Corbusier 7, 22, 23, 26-28, 30, 31, 54,
    55, 57-59, 92, 121, 135 136, 152
Ledwinka, Hans 81
Ledwinka, Joseph 148
Lefébvre, André 48, 49, 50, 53, 148
Léger, Fernand 19
Lengyel, Stefan 90
Lenoir, Jean Joseph Etienne 12
Leonardo da Vinci 11, 135
Lethaby, William Richard 24
Libeskind, Daniel 133
Lichtenstein, Roy 123
Lisker, R 45
Lissitzky, El 135
Loewy, Raymond 10, 20, 24, 34, 36, 81
Loos, Adolf 38, 42, 43, 65
Luder, Owen 131
Lutyens, Edwin 11, 12, 130
Lutzmann, Friedrich 33
Lux, Joseph-August 19
Lyall, John 131

160

Maillart, Robert 19, 20
Maillol, Aristide 25
Maldonaldo, Tomás 22
Malevich, Kasimir 135
Manrique, César 123, 124
Manser, Michael 131
Mantegazza, Francesco 107
Marinetti, Fillipo Tommaso 13, 14, 15, 134
Masselink, Eugene 36
Mather, Rick 131
Matté-Trucco, Giacomo 28
Maybach, Wilhelm 12
Mendelsohn, Erich 71, 128
Michelin, André and Edouard 48, 54
Mollino, Carlo 92-96
Mongermon, Eugène 54
Moore, Henry 26, 127
Morley, Christopher 83
'Moving Objects' 130
Mumford, Lewis 153
Munari, Bruno 120
Muratet, Jean 48
Museum of Contemporary Art, Sydney 106
Museum of Modern Art, New York 6, 24, 25, 65

Nardi, Enrico 92, 94-96
Neutra, Richard 65, 66
Nixon, David 102

Noël-Telmont, André Noël 54, 113
Novotny, Otakar 112

Olbrich, Joseph Maria 11, 33
Opron, Robert 122
Otto, Frei 120
Otto, Nikolaus August 12
Ozenfant, Amédée 22

Pagano, Giuseppe 62, 64, 84
Palmer, Gerald 127
Paolozzi, Eduardo 141
Paulon, D 45
Pawley, Martin 6
Pazzani, Alexander 11
Pearson, Philip 77, 82
Peters, William Wesley 30, 36
Pevsner, Antoine 135
Phillips, Alan 130
Piano, Renzo 7, 107-111, 146
Picabia, Francis 15
Pingusson, Georges-Henri 115, 116
Pininfarina 24
Plan Voisin 54
Pollock, Jackson 16
Ponti, Gio 28, 62-64, 84
Poulain, Hervé 123
Pringle, Jack 131
Prouvé, Jean 88, 89

Rachlis, M 45
Rauschenberg, Robert 123
Read, Herbert 19, 20, 127
Revelli de Beaumont, Mario 59
Rice, Peter 7, 107-111
Richards, J M 21
Rietveld, Gerrit Thomas 113, 114
Robie, Fred C 136
Rock, David 131
Rodin, Auguste 25
Rogers, Richard 146
Rosselli, Alberto 28
Rottier, Guy 121
Royce, Henry 130
Rudolph, Paul 152
Rumpler, Edmund 44, 80

Sainsbury, Robert and Lisa 97
Sainturat, Maurice 49
Sanders, Walter 82
Sant'Elia, Antonio 134, 135

Sason, Sixten 64
Scaglione, Franco 20, 21
Schaeffer, Rodolfo 59
Schein, Ionel 141, 142
Schindler, Rudolph 65, 66
Severini, Gino 26
Siddeley, John 59
Slapeta, Lubomír 118
Smithson, Alison and Peter 141, 143
Solomon R Guggenheim Museum, New York 137
Sottsass, Ettore 120
Spengler, Oswald 71, 72
Stam, Mart 90
Starck, Philippe 123, 125, 126
Steinbeck, John 16
Stella, Frank 123
Stieglitz, Alfred 15
Stirling, James 131
Stout, William B 81
Strong, Gordon 137

Tait, Thomas Smith 60
Tarza, Tristan 44
Tatlin, Vladimir 135
Taylor, Frederick Winslow 136
Teague, Walter Dorwin 10
'Ten Automobiles' 7, 24, 25
Tjaarda, John 36
Townsend, John 131
Trevithick, Richard 12
Turner, Richard 101

Übelacker, Erich 81

Velde, Henry van de 13, 128
Venturi, Robert 31
Verne, Jules 10
Voisin, Gabriel 54, 113

Wagner, Otto 65, 112
Webb, Michael 146, 147
Wells, H G 80
Wright, Frank Lloyd 8, 28, 29, 30, 31, 33, 34,
    36-41, 71, 112, 128, 130, 131, 136-139
Wright, John 33

Yorke, F R S 24

Zeppelin airships 81